Foundations for Efficient Web Service Selection

Qi Yu • Athman Bouguettaya

Foundations for Efficient Web Service Selection

Foreword by Fabio Casati

 Springer

Qi Yu
College of Computing and
Information Sciences
Rochester Institute of Technology
1 Lomb Memorial Drive
Rochester, NY 14623-5603
USA
qi.yu@rit.edu

Athman Bouguettaya
CSIRO ICT Center
Computer Sci. & Information Tech. Bldg.
North Road
Canberra, ACT 2601
Australia
athman.bouguettaya@csiro.au

ISBN 978-1-4419-0313-6   e-ISBN 978-1-4419-0314-3
DOI 10.1007/978-1-4419-0314-3
Springer New York Dordrecht Heidelberg London

Library of Congress Control Number: 2009933095

Printed on acid-free paper

Springer is part of Springer Science+Business Media (www.springer.com)

To my wife Xumin and my daughter Emily for their love, encouragement, and support.

Qi Yu

To my wife Malika and my three children Zakaria, Ayoub, and Mohamed-Islam.

Athman Bouguettaya

Foreword

The problem of search in Web services has been attracting the attention of researchers over the last decade. The reason for this is that as service technology evolves and as more services become available (and even more now with the advent of *cloud computing*) it becomes important to be able to locate the service that meets our needs within a large and sometimes dense cloud of offering. Many, often "spot" proposals have been put forward to address the problem and several standards have been defined, but none of these has been effective or is now accepted as the way to perform service search.

This excellent book looks at the search problem from a broader perspective. Instead of narrowing down on a specific aspect or subproblem of service search, it dissects and analyzes the fundamental problems in search and presents concrete, applicable solutions as well as the theoretical foundations behind them. In particular, Yu and Bouguettaya define the notion and the characteristics of a Web Services Management System, which is the service analogous of a DBMS. They define why a WSMS is needed, and what makes it similar to and different from a DBMS. They specify a service model and a service algebra for querying Web services. All these aspects denote a rigorous and holistic approach to the problem which not only supports the search techniques provided in the book but that can be used as an underlying framework for researchers to come.

One aspect I found particularly significant in the book is the mind shift it generates from thinking about service modeling for the sake of supporting deployment or invocation to modeling for supporting search. This *design for search* approach is exactly what we do when we design databases because search is what we worry about in that case, and there is no reason why this shouldn't be the case for services if we want services to be searchable with a similar effectiveness.

Among the other many goodies that you will be able to appreciate reading Yu's and Bouguettaya's book there are two in particular which stroke my attention and that I would like to single out: the first is the quality-oriented approach to search and within this the ability of the system to support users in the tedious and often impossible task to select weights for quality properties. This will be key in making service search viable. The second, an issue I have rarely seen discussed at all, is the importance of searching services assuming that information is uncertain. This topic is picking up in database management but it is even more important in service management as data from services — especially quality description data — is by its very nature uncertain, and handling this is fundamental for the success of a service search paradigm. I hope you enjoy reading this book as much as I had.

Fabio Casati

Preface

The Web has evolved to encompass various information resources accessible worldwide. Organizations across all spectra have already moved their main operations to the Web, which has brought about a fast growth of various Web applications. Service oriented computing is emerging as a new computing paradigm for efficient deployment and access of these exponentially growing plethora of Web applications. The development of enabling technologies for such an infrastructure is expected to change the way of conducting business on the Web. Web services have become de facto the most significant technological by-product.

The ability to efficiently access Web services is necessary, in light of the large and widely geographically disparate space of services. Using Web services would typically consist of invoking their operations by sending and receiving messages. However, complex applications, for example, a travel package that accesses multiple Web services, would need an integrated framework to efficiently access and manipulate Web services functionalities. The increasing adoption of Web services requires a systematic support of query facilities. The service oriented queries would enable users to access multiple Web services in a transparent and efficient manner. In addition, as Web services with similar functionality are expected to be provided by competing providers, a major challenge is devising optimization strategies for finding the best Web services or composition thereof with respect to the expected user-supplied quality (e.g., time, fee, and reputation).

The existing standards-based service discovery technologies are clearly insufficient for building a full-fledged service query infrastructure. Current Web service search engines or service registries (e.g., UDDI) mainly support simple keyword-based search on Web services. However, this keyword search paradigm cannot always precisely locate Web services partially because of the rich semantics embodied in these services. Query processing on Web services is a novel concept that goes beyond the traditional data-centric view of query processing, which is mainly performance centered. It focuses on user-quality parameters to select multiple services that are equivalent in functionality but exhibit different Quality of Web service (QoWS).

In this book, we describe a novel foundational framework that lays out a theoretical underpinning for the emerging service computing. The proposed framework provides disciplined and systematic support for efficient access to Web services' functionalities. The key components of the proposed framework centers around a novel service model that provides a formal abstraction of the Web services within an application domain. A service calculus and a service algebra are defined to facilitate users in accessing services via declarative service queries. We provide the implementation of the service algebra. This enables the generation of Service Execution Plans (SEPs) that can be used by users to directly access services. We present an optimization algorithm to efficiently select the SEPs with the best QoWS. We then propose a multi-objective optimization approach that releases users from the tedious weight assigning process. We develop service skyline computation techniques that return a set of most interesting SEPs. The service skyline guarantees to include the user desired SEPs. We further explore a set of novel heuristics for computing service skylines over sets of services. This enables users to efficiently and optimally access multiple services simultaneously as an integrated service package. Finally, we consider the performance fluctuation of service providers due to the dynamic service environment. We propose an uncertain QoWS model and a novel concept called p-dominant service skyline. We develop new indexing structures and algorithms to efficiently compute the p-dominant service skyline. We derive analytical models and conduct extensive sets of experiments to evaluate the proposed framework and service query optimization algorithms.

Qi Yu
Athman Bouguettaya

Acknowledgements

I would like to thank my parents for their all time love and support. My most special thanks go to my wife, Xumin. It is her love, dedication, and endless support that made me reach this far. I am also indebted to my daughter, Emily, who brought the sunshine into my busiest life when preparing this book.

Qi Yu

I would like to acknowledge the support of my family during the preparation of this book: my wife Malika, my children: Zakaria, Ayoub, and Mohamed-Islam. I would also like to thank my employer CSIRO (Australia) for providing me the environment to successfully finish this work.

Athman Bouguettaya

Contents

Chapter 1
Introduction

The Web is a distributed, dynamic, and large information repository. It has now evolved to encompass various information resources accessible worldwide. Organizations across all spectra have already moved their main operations to the Web, which has brought about a fast growth of various Web applications. This has dramatically increased the need to build a fundamental infrastructure for efficient deployment and access of the exponentially growing plethora of Web applications. The development of enabling technologies for such an infrastructure is expected to change the business paradigm on the Web. *Web services* have become *de facto* the most significant technological by-product. Simply put, a Web service is a piece of software application whose interface and binding can be defined, described, and discovered as XML artifacts [4]. It supports direct interactions with other software agents using XML-based messages exchanged via Internet-based protocols. Examples of Web services include online reservation, ticket purchase, stock trading, and auction. Standards are key enablers of Web services [83]. Major industry players took a lead to set up crucial standards. This has greatly facilitated the adoption and deployment of Web services [48]. Three key XML-based standards have been defined to support Web service deployment: SOAP [85], WSDL [87], and UDDI [58]. SOAP defines a communication protocol for Web services. WSDL enables service providers to describe their applications. UDDI offers a registry service that allows advertisement and discovery of Web services.

The fast increasing number of Web services is transforming the Web from a *data-oriented* repository to a *service-oriented* repository [65, 72]. In this anticipated framework, existing business logic will be wrapped as Web services that would be accessible on the Web via a Web service middleware [84]. Web services will work as self-contained entities to fulfill users' requests. Cooperation among multiple Web services will additionally improve the *quality* of answers by providing *value-added* services [55]. Web services are anticipated to form the underlying technology that will realize the envisioned "sea of services" [65].

Q. Yu and A. Bouguettaya, *Foundations for Efficient Web Service Selection*,
DOI 10.1007/978-1-4419-0314-3_1, © Springer Science+Business Media, LLC 2009

1.1 Web Service Foundation

Web services have been so far mainly driven by standards. They have yet to have a solid theoretical underpinning. The foundational work is still in its infancy. Providing a solid framework for Web services aims at providing a powerful foundation much like the relational paradigm provided for the database field. In the context of Web services, scientific communities are expected to benefit from the ability to share resources on a large scale that will lead to further innovation, collaboration, and discovery. Governments would be able to better serve citizens and other constituencies by streamlining and combining their Web accessible resources. Businesses would be able to dynamically outsource their core functionalities and provide economies of scale. This would translate into better products at cheaper prices.

Fully delivering on the potential of the next-generation Web services requires building a foundation that would provide a sound design framework for the entire life cycle of Web services, including efficiently developing, deploying, publishing, discovering, composing, monitoring, and optimizing access to Web services. The proposed Web service foundation will enable the deployment of *Web Service Management Systems* (WSMSs) that would be to Web services what DBMSs have been to data. We largely draw on the experience and lessons learned from designing the database foundation. The transition from the early file systems to databases is of particular interest. If one looks carefully at the history of relational databases, one can clearly observe a striking parallel with the current situation of Web services. Therefore, understanding the related transition processes and resulting foundational models will provide us with valuable insight and help in designing a sound foundational framework for Web services.

1.1.1 Historical Perspective

For the purpose of comparison, it is noteworthy to mention that the early file systems were developed for single users who had their own exclusive data space. In addition, because of the state of data storage technology back then, data sizes were very small. Computer systems were more computation bound (CPU bound) as opposed to being data bound (I/O bound). More importantly, the growing deployment of computer systems was coupled with a tremendous growth in data volume and number of users sharing files. The new computing environment posed fundamental challenges in providing uniform data representation, efficient *concurrent* access to and recoverability of data, and ensuring *correctness* and *consistency*. As a result, the nascent database research focused on laying the foundation for the next-generation data management system to address these issues. Early work on the network and hierarchical models set the foundational work in motion with the early standardization-based models (e.g. DBTG model [2, 1]). The field of databases enjoyed widespread acceptance only after the relational model was proposed by Codd [27]. What made the relational model a success story is the sound mathematical foundation upon which it is built. The relational model is based on set theory and relational calculus (declarative). This simple, yet powerful paradigm was met with instant success in industry [5] and academia [77]. New concurrency control models were proposed. Optimization techniques based on algebraic principles were also proposed. This activity spurred and sustained the deployment of databases as ubiquitous tools for efficiently managing large amounts of data.

We observe that this historical perspective on managing data is quite similar with the evolution of Web services. Web services deliver complex functionalities over the Web. The early function libraries (e.g., DLL on Windows) were also designed to wrap certain functionalities and make them reusable. The libraries provide a set of APIs, upon which users can manually incorporate the functionalities into their programs. In addition, function libraries are only locally accessible. The emergence of computer networks present new requirements for functionalities sharing and reusing. There is a need to integrate applications within or across organizations. Middleware technologies (e.g., RPC, COM, and CORBA) took a first step to support intra-organization interoperability. Web services came as a result to address the inter-organization interoperability. They aim to provide users an integrated access to the functionalities available on the Web. The development of Web services has so far mostly been the result of standardization bodies usually operating on a consensus basis and driven by market considerations. In this context, innovation and long term market effects are not usually primary concerns. Because of the global nature of the Web, the standardization process has so far been very fragmented, leading to competing and potentially incompatible Web service infrastructures. Many companies have invested very heavily in Web services technologies (Microsoft's .NET, IBM's Websphere, SUN's J2EE, to name a few). These efforts have resulted in a fast-growing number of Web services being made available. The envisioned business model is expected to include a whole community of Web service providers that will compete to provide Web services. It is important that this investment produces the expected results. To maximize the benefits of this new technology, there is a need to provide a sound and clean methodology for specifying, selecting, optimizing, and composing Web services. This needs to take place within a secure environment. The underlying foundation will enable designers and developers to reason about Web services to produce efficient Web Service Management Systems.

1.1.2 Web Services vs. Data

Despite similarities in nature and history, Web services are different from data in many significant ways. First, data in traditional DBMSs are passive objects with a set of known properties, e.g., structure, value, functional dependencies, integrity constraints. On the other hand, Web services are active and autonomous entities that have a set of *functions* rather than *values*. Moreover, unlike data in DBMSs, Web services may exhibit some run-time *behavior* when they are invoked. Second, accessing a service on the Web is similar to accessing data from a distributed DBMS. For example, to access a Web service, the service requester must search in one or more service registries. However, Web services carry more complex information, which makes accessing services a more complicated process. This involves understanding the different services' syntactic and semantic descriptions, selecting the services providing the requested functionality, understanding their communication protocols, and finally engaging in a sequence of message exchange with the selected services. Of significant importance are more complex scenarios where requests for services may require the composition of several Web services; various issues pertaining to individual Web services need to be reconciled before they can be combined.

1.1.3 Service Query Optimization

The ability to efficiently access Web services is necessary, in light of the large and widely geographically disparate service space. In addition, as Web services with similar functionality are expected to be provided by competing providers, a major challenge is devising optimization strategies for finding the "best" Web services or composition thereof with respect to the expected user-supplied quality.

Example 1.1. Consider a Map *Web service that provides geographical information. Some typical operations offered by this services include:*

    op_1: GeoCode
      Input : Address [String]
      Output : Point [double lat, double long]
    op_2 : GetMap
      Input : Point [double lat, double long]
      Output : Map [URL]
    op_3 : GetTraffic
      Input : Point [double lat, double long]
      Output : TrafficReport [URL]

Assume that there are two service providers, S_1 and S_2 (e.g., Yahoo, Google), providing the same map service but with different user-centered qual-

ity that may include the response time, fee, and reputation (e.g., updating the delicacy of map). Suppose that a driver wants to view the map of the destination address she will drive to. She may first select op_2 to get the map. However, op_2 depends on op_1 to transform the user provided address to its required latitude and longitude. After the driver connects to S_1 and gets the map, she may find that the map is not up to date. In this case, she has to connect to S_2 to get a probably better map. ∎

Example 1.2. Suppose a user wants to do a trip planning. Typical Web services that need to be accessed include TripPlanner, *the* Map *service mentioned in Example 1.1, and some other services, like* Weather. TripPlanner *provides basic trip information, such as airlines, hotels, and things to do at destination. Other than this, users may also be interested to see the city map, local attractions, etc, by accessing the* Map *service. The weather condition during the travel days is another important factor that makes the* Weather *service a primary interest.* ∎

From the above two examples, we note that efficient and optimal access to Web services' functionalities usually goes beyond simple operation invocation via sending and receiving messages. In addition to following the dependency constraints (e.g., op_2 depends on op_1 in Example 1.1) to access service operations, users typically want to get access to a service provider with their desired quality from multiple competing ones (like S_1 and S_2 in Example 1.1). However, this usually requires a series of trial-run processes and would be very painstaking if the number of competing providers is large. Things may become more complicated if users need to access multiple services at the same time, like the trip planning in Example 1.2. To get a desired trip package, users need to give a holistic consideration with respect to the quality of the service package, such as the overall response time, fee, and reputation. The possible combinations of providers for each service will far exceed the range for a manual selection by the users. Therefore, disciplined optimization strategies are required for finding the "best" Web services or composition thereof with respect to the *Quality of Web Services (QoWS)*.

1.2 Major Issues in Building a Web Service Foundation

The proliferation of Web services is forming a large service space, which still keeps growing. However, there is no holistic view about how to organize, manipulate, and access the large number of services. This triggers the need for an integrated infrastructure that can provide a systematic support on Web services. The existing enabling technologies for Web services are still not sufficient to fulfill the above requirement. For example, current Web service search engines or service registries mainly support simple keyword-based search on Web services. However, this keyword search paradigm may not be sufficient for locating Web services partially because of the rich semantics embodied in these services. Things may become more challenging when services are programmatically integrated into more complex applications (e.g., travel package, navigation system) through service composition. Since service operations with the same input-output types may provide totally different functionalities [32], more precise and reliable search mechanisms are required to locate the right services and ensure that the composed services can provide the desired functionality. Furthermore, even the desired services are successfully located, invoking services may not be that straightforward. There may be *implicit dependency constraints* between different service operations. The constraints may require that the invocation of some service operations occur only after their dependent operations have been successfully invoked. Users may have to browse the entire service description to explore these constraints before being able to invoke the service operations.

The ability to locate, compose, and invoke services only partially addresses the issues. The growing number of Web services gives users more options because multiple service providers may compete to offer the same functionality. However, it also brings users another problem: selecting a proper provider with the desired quality of service. Typically, users have to go through a series of trial-run processes. It would be even more painstaking if users want to target the providers that *best* suit their preference. Therefore, the user may want to include the quality requirement into the search criteria. In this case, it is necessary to differentiate competing Web services based on user expected QoWS.

The objective of this research is to provide a formal framework for enabling Web service query optimization. We focus on giving Web services a solid theoretical foundation. This will serve as a key block for building tomorrow's WSMS.

We summarize the challenging issues that need to be dealt with while building the foundational framework for service query optimization.

R1:   *Web services modeling.* In traditional relational database systems, data schema is used to describe and organize a large amount of data instances, which allows efficient and systematic query on the data space. As a prerequisite to query Web services, there is a need to provide an efficient and "meaningful" framework to organize Web services. This is especially important and desirable due to the large and heterogeneous service space. Web services should be modeled in a way that can capture their key features to filter interactions and accelerate service searches. The service model can also provide the language constructs for the service queries.

R2:   *Querying Web services.* Service queries are different from the traditional data queries because the first class objects retrieved are no longer the simple data items. Instead, a service query would help users retrieve services based on their functionalities. Users' requirements on non-functional properties (i.e., QoWS) of the services must also be captured by the service queries. In addition, dependency constraints may exist between different service operations. These constraints should be referred to when a service query retrieves the service operations that are dependent on other operations. For example, the output of some service operations might serve as the input of another service operation. Therefore, the latter service operation would depend on the execution of the former service operation. Thus, when the latter service operation is retrieved by a service query, the first one should be automatically retrieved because of this dependency relationship. Users should be able to formulate *declarative* service queries by only specifying the required functionality and quality without worrying about the internal dependency constraints.

R3: *QoWS aware service query optimization.* Traditional query optimization technologies are mainly "performance centered", aiming to produce efficient query plans. However, having an efficient query plan is still not sufficient in optimizing Web service queries. The query plan could retrieve multiple service execution plans, which are equivalent in terms of functionality and behavior. For example, an efficient query plan may return many service execution plans that fulfill Mary's requirements in terms of functionality and behavior. However, they may provide different quality of service, such as fees, reliability, and reputation etc. Since Mary may have special requirement on the quality of service, she still needs to manually select the one with the best quality. Therefore, the service query optimization should be able to efficiently process the query and generate the service execution plan with the best QoWS at the same time.

R4: *Dealing with multiple and conflicting quality parameters.* Existing service optimization approaches usually select services based on a predefined objective function [59, 94]. They require users to express their preference over different (and sometimes conflicting) quality parameters as numeric *weights*. The objective function assigns a scalar value to each service provider based on the quality values and the weights given by the service user. The provider gaining the highest value from the objective function will be selected and returned to the user. Implementing such an optimization strategy may pose two major issues: (i) Transforming personal preferences to numeric weights is a rather demanding task for users. (ii) Users may lose the flexibility to select their desired providers by themselves.

R5: *Service Query Optimization over Uncertain QoWS.* Current service optimization approaches assume that the quality delivered by service providers do not change over time. In addition, the QoWS values may not precisely reflect the actual performance of a service provider. First, the performance of a service provider may fluctuate due to the dynamic service environment. For example, the response time may vary due to the quality of the network. Second, service providers may not always deliver according to their "promised" quality because of "intentional" deceptions. Therefore, the actual QoWS delivered by service providers is inherently uncertain. Selecting service providers based on the advertised QoWS values does not capture the inherent uncertainty of the actual QoWS.

1.2.1 Summary of Contributions

We present a novel foundational framework that lays out a theoretical underpinning for the emerging services science. The proposed framework provides
disciplined support that enables users to efficiently access services with their
best desired quality in a transparent manner. It systematically addresses
each of the above research issues. More precisely, the major contributions are
summarized as follows:

C1: *Foundational service framework.* We develop a foundational service
     framework that is expected to layout a theoretical underpinning for the
     deployment of Web Service Management Systems (WSMSs). The key com-
     ponents of this framework centers around a formal *service model* that cap-
     tures the three key features of Web services: *functionality, behavior*, and
     quality. Functionality is specified by the operations offered by a Web ser-
     vice. Behavior reflects how the service operations can be invoked. It is
     decided by the dependency constraints between service operations. Qual-
     ity determines the non-functional properties of a Web service. We pro-
     pose a *service calculus* based on the service model. Service queries can be
     declaratively specified as calculus expressions. We propose a *service alge-
     bra* consisting of a set of algebraic operators. A calculus service query can
     be transformed into an equivalent algebraic expression. A set of algebraic
     equivalent rules is also derived to transform user provided algebraic ex-
     pression into the ones that can be more efficiently processed by the query
     processor. We develop a set of algorithms to efficiently implement the al-
     gebraic operators. The *physical implementation* of these operators enables
     to generate Service Execution Plans (SEPs) that can be directly used by
     users to access services.
C2: *QoWS aware service query optimization.* The traditional data query
     optimization techniques are usually system-centered with the major focus
     on improving the performance. The service query optimization problem
     poses new challenges. Due to the competition between a possibly large
     number of service providers, multiple SEPs can be generated from a service
     query. These SEPs all satisfy the functional requirement of the user but
     are different from each other in terms of QoWS. Since users may have
     specific preferences over different quality aspects, they still need to go
     through a series of trial-run process to get their desired SEP. We develop
     an algorithm which directly extends the dynamic programming approach
     for database query optimization. We then propose a divide-and-conquer
     algorithm, which is empowered by a greedy local search strategy that
     greatly improves the performance and also guarantees the quality of the
     obtained SEP.
C3: *Multi-objective service query optimization.* We propose the approach of
     multi-objective service query optimization through skyline computation.
     A skyline of SEPs (called *service skyline*) consists of a set of SEPs that

are not *dominated* by others. For example, SEP ϕ dominates SEP μ if ϕ is better than μ in at least one quality aspect and as good as or better than μ in all other aspects. We develop two algorithms for computing the service skyline: BBS4SEP and OGI. The former extends an efficient database skyline algorithm whereas the latter is based on a novel indexing structure constructed directly upon SEPs. Analytical and experimental results justify that OGI outperforms BBS4SEP under various parameter settings.

C4: *Skyline computation over sets of services.* Service users may want to access sets of services as an integrated service package (e.g., a travel package). However, computing a service skyline over sets of services (referred to as multi-service skyline) in a brute force manner incurs prohibitive computation cost. This is because the size of the SEP space increases exponentially with the number of services. We propose a set of heuristics to prune a large number of SEPs. We develop efficient algorithms that can scale to a large number of services.

C5: *Computing service skyline from uncertain QoWS.* We introduce the notion of *p-dominant service skyline* as an effective tool that facilitates service users in selecting their desired service providers with the presence of uncertainty in their QoWS. Specifically, a provider S belongs to the p-dominant service skyline if the chance that S is dominated by any other provider is less than p, where $p \in [0, 1]$, is a probability threshold. *By setting an appropriate probability threshold p, service users will gain a corresponding level of confidence (in terms of probability) that a selected provider "actually" belongs to the service skyline.* Thus, computing service skylines from uncertain QoWS provides a more meaningful and practical solution for the service optimization problem. We present a p-R-tree indexing structure and a dual-pruning scheme to efficiently compute the p-dominant service skyline.

We summarize in Table 1.1 how our contributions address each of the above research issues. We also list the chapters that cover the corresponding research contributions.

Table 1.1 Mapping between contributions and research issues

Contributions	Research issues	Chapters
C1	R1, R2	Chapter 3
C2	R3	Chapter 3
C3	R4	Chapter 4
C4	R4	Chapter 5
C5	R5	Chapter 6

1.3 Preview of Chapters

The book is organized into eight chapters and a preview of these chapters are given as follows.

In Chapter 2, we present an in-depth study of the enabling technologies for deploying and managing Web services. We propose a framework that identifies a set of dimensions to study and compare these technologies. We propose the architecture of the expected WSMS and investigate how each of these technologies can fit into this architecture. This also helps illustrate the role of the proposed service query optimization framework in enabling the deployment of the WSMS.

In Chapter 3, we present the foundational service framework. We elaborate on each of the key components in this framework, which consists of the service model, the service calculus, the service algebra, and the service query optimizer. An QoWS aware optimization algorithm is developed that extends the dynamic programming approach to efficiently select the SEPs with the best user-desired quality.

In Chapter 4, we present a multi-objective service query optimization approach that releases service users from weight assignment during the optimization process. We propose a novel concept, called service skyline, that consists of a set of most interesting SEPs. The service skyline guarantees to include the user desired SEPs. We develop two algorithms to compute the service skyline.

In Chapter 5, we present efficient and scalable algorithms to compute service skylines over sets of services. This is motivated by the fact that a straightforward application of skyline algorithms in Chapter 3 to a large number of service will incur prohibitive computation cost. We first present a one pass algorithm based on the observation that a multi-service skyline is completely determined by the single service skylines. The skyline can be returned after a complete enumeration on a significantly reduced candidate space. We then develop a dual progressive algorithm that is completely pipelineable and able to progressively report the skyline. We extend the dual progressive algorithm through an early pruning strategy and develop a scalable bottom up approach that performs with a nearly optimal time complexity.

In Chapter 6, we present a novel concept, called p-dominant service skyline to deal with the uncertainty in the QoWS. A provider S belongs to the p-dominant skyline if the chance that S is dominated by any other provider is less than p. We present a p-R-tree indexing structure and a dual-pruning scheme to efficiently compute the p-dominant skyline.

In Chapter 7, we present the related works that are most related to our research. This helps differentiate the proposed research with existing efforts from service computing and database research.

In Chapter 8, we provide concluding remarks and discuss directions for future research.

Chapter 2
Towards a WSMS: The State of the Art

A variety of definitions about Web services are given by different industry leaders, research groups, and Web service consortia. For example, the W3C consortium defines a Web service as *"a software system designed to support interoperable machine-to-machine interaction over a network. It has an interface described in a machine-processable format (specifically WSDL). Other systems interact with the Web service in a manner prescribed by its description using SOAP messages, typically conveyed using HTTP with an XML serialization in conjunction with other Web-related standards"* [88]. IBM defines Web services as *"self-describing, self-contained, modular applications that can be mixed and matched with other Web services to create innovative products, processes, and value chains. Web services are Internet applications that fulfill a specific task or a set of tasks that work with many other web services in a manner to carry out their part of a complex workflow or a business transaction"*. According to Microsoft, *"A Web Service is a unit of application logic providing data and services to other applications. Applications access Web Services via ubiquitous Web protocols and data formats such as HTTP, XML, and SOAP, with no need to worry about how each Web Service is implemented"*. HP defines Web services as *"modular and reusable software components that are created by wrapping a business application inside a Web service interface. Web services communicate directly with other web services via standards-based technologies"*. SUN perceives a Web service as an *"application functionality made available on the World Wide Web. A Web service consists of a network-accessible service, plus a formal description of how to connect to and use the service"*.

The aforementioned definitions give a high-level description of the major objective and supporting technologies of Web services. Interoperation among machines is the major design goal of Web services. As the supporting standards, WSDL enables XML service description of Web services and SOAP defines a communication protocol for Web services. These definitions give an *outside* view of Web services. In this section, we go a step further by setting up a comprehensive WSMS framework to support the entire Web service

Q. Yu and A. Bouguettaya, *Foundations for Efficient Web Service Selection,*
DOI 10.1007/978-1-4419-0314-3_2, © Springer Science+Business Media, LLC 2009

life cycle, including *developing, deploying, publishing, discovering, composing, monitoring,* and *optimizing* access to Web services. The remainder of
this chapter is organized as follows. We first describe a scenario that will be
used as an running example throughout this chapter in Section 2.1. We then
present the Web service reference model in Section 2.2. We elaborate on the
three key players in this model. We also identify different layers that enable
the interaction in the Web service model in Section 2.3. We define a collection
of dimensions across these layers in Section 2.4. The major components of
the proposed WSMS are devised based on these dimensions. Each component
provides functionalities that address the issues specified by the corresponding dimension. Finally, we present the architecture of the proposed WSMS
in Section 2.5.

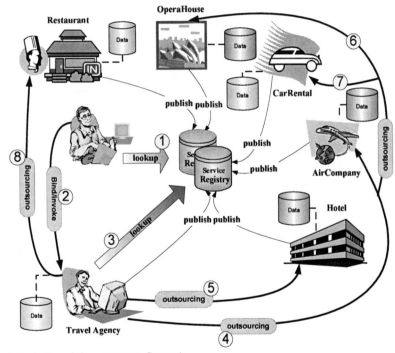

Fig. 2.1 A Travel Arrangement Scenario

2.1 Scenario

We consider a travel agency, named `TravelAgency`, providing the travel
arrangement (e.g., transportation, itinerary, and accommodations) for its
clients (Figure 2.1). Assume a university professor, Joan, wants to attend
an international conference in Sydney, Australia. Typical services needed by

Joan might include airlines, ground-transportation (e.g., taxi and car rental), accommodation (e.g., hotels and inns), and other entertainment services (e.g., restaurant and opera house). Joan needs to first search for the services that provide travel packages. The search can be conducted in some well-known service registry. We assume that `TravelAgency` is located by Joan. Joan would then send her request to it. To offer a complete tour package, `TravelAgency` needs support from its business partners (e.g., `AirCompany`, `Hotel`, `Restaurant`, `CarRental`, and `OperaHouse`) to arrange flights, hotels, cars, and other entertainment facilities. These companies all define the service description for their Web services and publish them on a well-known service registry, whereby `TravelAgency` can search and locate them. `TravelAgency` needs to outsource services from these business partners to provide the entire travel package. Since Web services with similar functionalities might be provided by competing business partners, there is a need to optimize access those Web services or composition thereof with respect to the expected quality. In addition, the Web services need to be accessed in a reliable and secure manner. This example articulates a typical Web service usage scenario. It will serve as a running example to illustrate various Web service concepts.

2.2 Web Service Reference Model

Three types of participants cooperate to set up a Web service model (see Figure 2.2), including: *service provider, service client*, and *service registry*. Web services interact in three primary modes: *service publishing, finding*, and *binding*. Interactions depend on the Web service *artifacts*, which include the *service implementation* and the *service description*.

- *Participants* in a Web services model are categorized into three types:
  - *Service provider* is the owner of the Web services. It holds the implementation of the service application and makes it accessible via the Web.
  - *Service client* represents a human or a software agent that intends to make use of some services to achieve a certain goal.
  - *Service registry* is a searchable registry providing service descriptions. It implements a set of mechanisms to facilitate service providers to publish their service descriptions. Meanwhile, it also enables service clients to locate services and get the binding information.

- *Interactions* with a Web service take place in three modes:
  - *Service publication* is to make the service description available in the registry so that the service client can find it.
  - *Service lookup* is to query the registry for a certain type of service and then retrieve the service description.

– *Service binding* is to locate, contact, and invoke the service based on the binding information in the service description.

• *Artifacts* encompass the service implementation and description:

– *Service implementation* is a network accessible software module realized by the service provider. It could be invoked by a service client or act as a service client to interact with another service provider.

– *Service description* could contain the syntactic and semantic information of the Web services. The syntactic information describes the input/output of the operations, the binding information, the data types, and so on. The semantic information encompasses the domain of interests, business functionalities, QoWS issues, and so on.

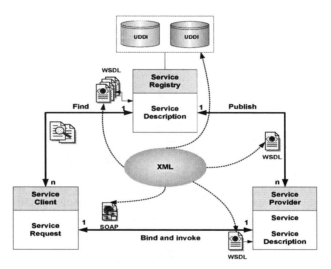

Fig. 2.2 W3C Web Services Reference Model

2.3 Web Service Stack

The Web service stack contains five key layers: communications, messaging, descriptions, discovery, and processes, which are shown along the vertical direction in Figure 2.3. It is an extension of the W3C service stack [88]. Similar to the W3C service stack, each stack layer provides certain functionality to support interoperation between Web services and service clients or among Web services. However, we categorize interoperability into two dimensions: syntactic and semantic (see Section 2.4 for details). Therefore, our service stack is distinguished from the W3C stack by further identifying the syntactic and semantic interoperability offered by all layers above the messaging layer.

- *Communications:* The underpinning of the Web services stack is the network, where the underlying communications take place. A set of network protocols help realize the network accessibility of Web services. The wide adoption of HTTP makes it the first choice of standard network protocol for Internet available Web services. Other network protocols could also be supported, such as SMTP.
- *Messaging:* The messaging layer provides a document-based messaging model for the interaction with Web services. The messaging model works with a wide variety of network protocols. For example, the messaging model can be combined with HTTP to traverse firewalls. In another case, combination with SMTP enables the interaction with Web services that support asynchronous message exchanges.
- *Description:* The description (or representation) layer is for describing Web services. It wraps Web services and specifies their functionalities, operations, data types, and binding information using a service interface. The WS discovery will rely on the WS representation to locate appropriate Web services.
- *Discovery:* The discovery layer is for locating and publishing Web services. It enables the usage of Web services in a much wider scale. Service providers can store the service descriptions in a service registry via the publication functionalities provided by WS discovery. Meanwhile, service requestors can query the service registry and look for interested services based on the stored service descriptions.
- *Processes:* The processes layer supports more complex interactions between Web services, which enables Web service interoperation. It relies on the basic interaction functionalities provided by the technologies at lower layers in the Web service stack. For example, it needs Web service discovery and representation for querying and locating Web services based on their descriptions. The selected Web services are used to construct the process, which consists of a sequence of coordinated Web services.

2.4 Key Dimensions for Building a WSMS

The variety of the Web service technologies constitutes a rich solution space of Web services. Each technology has specific design requirements depending on the usage scenarios. Therefore, it is important to determine the relevant requirements for deploying and managing Web services. In this section, we identify a set of dimensions to evaluate Web service technologies. These dimensions are in line with the key requirements for deploying and managing Web services. We take the Web service stack as a starting point and extend it to address the developing trends of Web service technologies. The dimensions are defined according to the vertical layers of the Web service stack (see

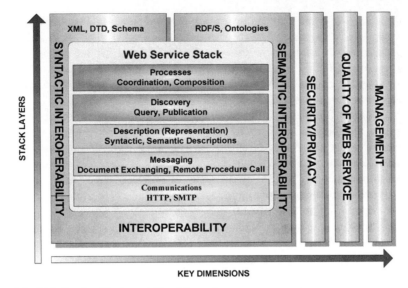

Fig. 2.3 Web Service Stack and Key Dimensions

Figure 2.3). They include *interoperability, security & privacy, Quality of Web Services (QoWS)*, and *management*.

Interoperability – This dimension refers to the extent to which participant Web services would cooperate to accomplish a common objective. For example, in the aforementioned scenario, `TravelAgency` needs to interoperate with `AirCompany` and `Hotel` to serve its clients. The common objective of the three parties is to provide satisfactory services for travelers. Good interoperability is a must for them to achieve this goal. Web services are designed to bring together applications from geographically distributed and heterogeneous environments and provide interoperability among them [73]. Interoperability could be achieved via three main approaches: *standards, ontology*, and *mediation*. A *standard* is a specification or format that has been approved by a recognized standardization organization or is accepted as a *de facto* standard by the industry. Several standardization efforts in Web services have been initiated by a focused group of companies, and have then been adopted by different organizations such as OASIS (Organization for the Advancement of Structured Standards) and W3C. These consortia aim at standardizing the different aspects of Web service interactions (e.g., message format, interaction protocols) [4]. An *ontology* is a *formal* and *explicit* specification of a *shared conceptualization* [30]. "Conceptualization" refers to an abstraction of a domain that identifies the relevant concepts in that domain. "Shared" means that an ontology captures *consensual* knowledge. The development of ontologies is often a cooperative process involving different entities possibly at different locations (e.g., businesses, government agencies). All entities that agree on using a given ontology commit themselves to the concepts and definitions within that ontology. "Explicit" means that the concepts used in an ontology and the constraints on their use are explicitly defined. "Formal" intends that the ontology should be machine understandable and describe using a well-defined model or language called *ontology language*. *Mediators* provide an integrated view or mediated schema over multiple heterogeneous and autonomous services [38]. This schema represents generally a synthesized view over a specific application domain. Users access the integrated view through a uniform interface. Each service is connected to a wrapper that enables its participation in the system. It translates between the services concepts and those at the mediator level.

Interoperability is the core functionality that Web services endeavors to achieve. Interoperation occurs at two levels: *syntactic* and *semantic*.

- *Syntactic interoperability* is concerned with the syntactic features of Web services. Examples of syntactic features include the number of parameters defining a message and the data types of those parameters. XML helps achieve syntactic interoperability by encoding syntactic information into XML documents. Additionally, XML provides platform and language independence, vendor neutrality, and extensibility, which are all crucial to interoperability.
- *Semantic interoperability* is the most challenging issue for achieving the truly seamless interoperation. It deals with semantic properties of Web services. Examples of semantic features include the domain of interest of a Web service and the functionality provided by an operation. The envisioned Semantic Web is is gaining momentum as the potential silver bullet for empowering Web services with semantics.

Interoperability could be achieved at different layers as depicted in Figure 2.3 [53]. *The communication layer* provides protocols for exchanging messages among remotely located partners (e.g., HTTP, SOAP). It is possible that partners use different proprietary communication protocols. In this case, gateways should be used to translate messages between heterogeneous protocols. The objective of interoperability at this layer is to achieve a seamless integration of the communication protocols. *The content (description) layer* provides languages and models to describe and organize information in such a way that it can be understood and used. Content interoperability requires that the involved systems understand the semantics of content and types of business documents. For instance, if a Web service receives a message that contains a document, it must determine whether the document represents a purchase order or request for quotation. Information translation, transformation, data mediators, and integration capabilities are needed to provide for reconciliation among disparate representations, vocabularies, and semantics. The objective of interoperability at this layer is to achieve a seamless integration of data formats, data models, and languages. *The process layer* is concerned with the conversational interactions (i.e, joint business process) among services. Before engaging in a transaction, service providers need to

agree on the procedures of their joint business process. The semantics of interactions among partners must be well defined, such that there is no ambiguity
as to what a message may mean, what actions are allowed, what responses
are expected, etc. The objective of interoperability at this layer is to allow autonomous and heterogeneous partners to come online, advertise their
terms and capabilities, and engage in peer-to-peer interactions with any other
partners. Examples of concepts for enabling process interoperability include
process wrappers and application adapters [17, 9].

Security & Privacy – Security is an important issue for deploying Web
services. Web services enable interoperation at the risk of letting outside in-
truders attack the internal applications and databases since they open up the
network to give access to outside users to these resources [35]. Web service
security needs to be concerned with the following aspects: *authentication, authorization, confidentiality,* and *integrity. Authentication* is used to verify a
claimed identity while *authorization* is to check whether a user is authorized
to perform a requested action. *Confidentiality* is to ensure that information
is disclosed only to authorized recipients by, for example encrypting the message. Lastly, *integrity* refers to the protection of the information from being
tampered with by, for example putting digital signatures on the messages.
Privacy is another major concern of Web service deployment [68]. During service interactions, personal data or business secrets (e.g., billing information,
shipping address, or product preference) might be unintentionally released
[3]. Conventional privacy protection mainly relies on law enforcement and restriction of social values. Emerging technologies for preserving privacy in Web
services include digital privacy credentials, data filters, and mobile privacy
preserving agents [68].

QoWS – The proliferation of Web services is expected to introduce compe-
tition among large numbers of Web services that offer similar functionalities.
The concept of QoWS is considered as a key feature in distinguishing between
competing Web services [84]. *QoWS* encompasses different quality parameters
that characterize the behavior of a Web service in delivering its functionalities. These parameters can be categorized into two major quality classes:
runtime quality and *business* quality. Quality parameters in these two classes
can be further extended to include more quality aspects of Web services to
fulfill the requirements of different application domains, such as *Accessibility,
Integrity,* and *Regulatory.*

Management – Web service management refers to the control and monitoring of Web service qualities and usage. Web service management mechanisms
are highly coupled with QoWS of a Web service. We identify two types of
management: *control* and *monitoring* management.

- *Control management* aims to improve the service quality through a set
  of control mechanisms. Typical control mechanisms include Web service
  transaction, Web service change management, and Web service optimization. Transactions help improve the reliability and fault-tolerance of Web
  services. Change management deals with highly dynamic environment of

Web services. It takes a series of actions to identify the changes, notifying the coupled entities, and adopting appropriate operations to response the change. Web service optimization helps users identify Web services and/or their combinations to best fulfill their requirements.

- *Monitoring management* rates the behavior of Web services in delivering its functionalities in terms of each QoWS parameter. Monitoring Web service behavior would be crucial in either calculating QoWS parameter values or assessing a Web service claim in terms of promised QoWS.

Control and monitoring management might sometimes work cooperatively. For instance, the Web service optimization would need the monitoring process to get the QoWS parameter values of different Web services and/or their combinations. These values would guide the optimization process to return the optimized solutions that best fulfill users' requirements.

2.5 The WSMS Architecture

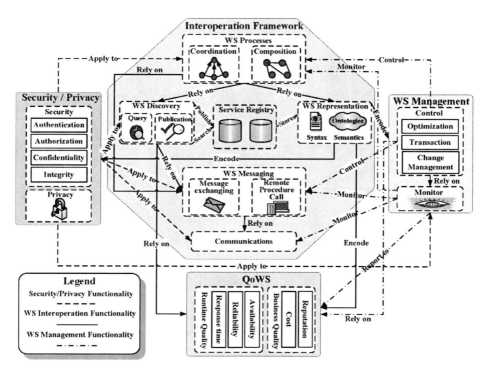

Fig. 2.4 The WSMS Architecture

In this section, we present the WSMS architecture. The design of the WSMS architecture leverages the research result in DBMSs. Web services will be treated and manipulated as first-class object in the proposed WSMS. The key components in this architecture are modeled after those in DBMSs. The functionality of each component aims to address the issues raised by the key dimensions. The interoperation framework consists of six subcomponents: communication, WS messaging, WS discovery, service registry, WS representation, and WS processes. The collaboration of these subcomponents provides mechanisms to efficient access and interoperation with Web services. The security/privacy component guarantees that the access and interoperation can be conducted in a secure and controlled manner. The QoWS component lays out a set of quality metrics that can be used to advertise and discover Web services. Some of the metrics can also be used to specify quality level agreement, such as payment, price, etc. The management component offers monitoring, transaction, change management, and optimization functionalities. The proposed WSMS provides value added features to enable reliable and optimized deployment of Web services. The architecture also reflects the relationship among different components. In what follows, we give a detailed description of the major functionality of each component.

The WS Interoperation Framework – The interoperation framework is at the core of the WSMS architecture. It addresses the interoperability issue of Web services through the collaboration of its six subcomponents. WS-messaging combines with an underlying communication protocol (e.g., HTTP and SMTP) to enable the basic interaction with Web services. A Web service takes the incoming message as the input to one of its methods and responds with the output of the method as a returning message. WS-representation defines the Web service interface containing a set of supported methods. It specifies the signature of each method, which is similar to IDL in the middleware systems. However, WS-representation goes beyond the IDL-like syntactic service description. It incorporates more expressive language constructs (e.g., ontologies) for describing the properties and capabilities of Web services in an unambiguous and computer-interpretable manner. Other information could also be specified in WS-representation, such as quality of service parameters, security and transaction requirements, etc. The semantic service description caters for the loosely-coupled interoperation between Web services. It helps Web services determine the functionality, requirement, and quality of their interoperation partners. Descriptions of Web services are stored at service registries. WS discovery provides the query and publication functionalities for locating and publishing Web services in a service registry. Interaction with the registry is through WS messaging. WS processes rely on the basic functionalities provided by the discovery, presentation, and messaging components to support the complex interactions between Web services. The processes involve the invocation of a sequence of Web services. Service coordination defines the external interaction protocols for a WS process whereas service composition defines the schemas for its internal implementation.

The WS Security/Privacy Component – The security/privacy component ensures that interactions with Web services are conducted in a secure fashion while sensitive information can be preserved as required. The security mechanisms need to be applied to all aspects of Web services, including messaging, query, publication, coordination, composition, control, and monitoring. Typical security functionalities that can be implemented by the security module are auditing, authentication, access control, and data encryption. Privacy is usually expressed by policies that reflect that the habits, behaviors, actions or other rights of the service users must be protected. Instead of relying on laws and social values, the privacy module enforces the policies from a technological perspective.

The QoWS Component – The QoWS component records the quality aspects of a Web service. It reflects the runtime and business requirements of Web services, such as response time, availability, reliability, cost, and reputation. Because it is anticipated that there will be multiple competitors to provide similar functionalities, the WS query process uses QoWS as a major criteria to select the "best" Web services. The QoWS component provides functionalities to define appropriate metrics to characterize *QoWS* and devise techniques to use it in optimizing service-based queries.

The WS Management Component – The WS management component is for monitoring and controlling the interactions with Web services. The monitoring module examines the behavior of the underlying communication, WS messaging, and WS processes and reports the runtime and business properties of Web services to the QoWS component. The control module provides transaction, optimization, and change management mechanisms to deliver the functionalities of Web services in a reliable, adaptive, and optimal fashion.

Figure 2.5 describes the proposed WSMS architecture using the W3C concept map model [88]. In this figure, rectangles represent concepts and lines with arrows represent relationships. The key components in the WSMS architecture are represented by the concepts. In addition to these key components, the concept map also includes the Web service (represented by WS) concept. The functionalities of each component are reflected by its relationships with the WS concept or other components.

The proposed WSMS provides a foundational framework for Web services. It formalizes the steps in the entire Web service life cycle. The design of each component in the WSMS architecture follows key research issues (called dimensions) in Web service environments. Since Web services are designed to achieve seamless interoperability, the interoperation framework stays at the core of the WSMS architecture. The framework is composed of several horizontally separated layers, each layer contains components that provide corresponding interoperation functionalities. The security/privacy, QoWS, and management components offer supplementary support (e.g., security, privacy, control, and monitoring) for the interoperation framework. These functionalities are orthogonal to the horizontal layers in the interoperation framework; they can be applied across these layers. This is different from the *Extended Service Oriented Architecture* (ESOA) [61]. ESOA contains three horizontal layers: basic service, service composition, and management layers. The sepa-

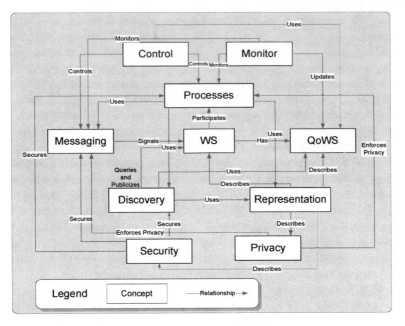

Fig. 2.5 A Concept-map Description of the WSMS Architecture

ration of different layers is based on the advancement of their functionalities. The basic service layer provides simple functionalities such as messaging, description, and discovery. The composition layer provides the functionalities for the consolidation of multiple service into a single composite service. The management layer provides advanced administration capacities for managing critical Web service based applications. Additionally, ESOA extends the *Service Oriented Architecture* (SOA) by addressing the new requirements introduced by Web services. The layers added in ESOA provide functionalities that overlap with existing SOA layers. However, the WSMS architecture is not developed by adding layers to an existing architecture. We take consideration of the key research issues of Web service when designing the WSMS architecture. Therefore, there is a clear functionality separation of different components in a WSMS.

In [62], Web service management approaches have been investigated to support production-quality Web service applications. The Web service management framework relies on a manageability information model and management infrastructure services to make Web services measurable and manageable. Specifically, the manageability information model describes the manageability information of Web services. Management infrastructure services define standard interfaces for the management functionalities, such as metering, monitoring, mediation, etc. We take an integrated approach and a broader scope to present the WSMS architecture. Management approaches investigated in [62] are complementary to those covered in the management component and fit into the the proposed WSMS architecture. There are some other research effort underway to provide architectural support for Web services such as Web Service Management Framework (WSMF) [33], Web Service Architecture (WSA) [88], Web Services Conceptual Architecture (WSCA) [43], Semantic Web enabled Web Services architecture (SWWS) [18], Service Bus [49], and Web Service Interoperability framework (WS-I) [90]. These architectures have addressed several similar components covered in our WSMS architecture. These components are designed to address the key research issues in the entire Web service life cycle. Unlike these architectures that present the components in an isolated manner, we take an integrated approach to investigate the functionalities of each component in the proposed WSMS architecture. We further examine the relationship between these components and how they could collaborate to set up the WSMS to enable the entire Web service life cycle including developing, deploying, publishing, discovering, composing, monitoring, and optimizing access to Web services.

Chapter 3
A Foundational Service Framework

Despite the proliferation of Web services, the field of service research is still in its infancy, where there has been little foundational work to date. In this chapter, we present the foundational service framework that helps address some fundamental research issues on Web services [44, 74]. The presented framework offers a systematic approach that enables users to achieve an optimal *Service Execution Plan (SEP)* by submitting declarative service queries. Figure 3.1 shows the overall architecture of the service query optimization framework. At the bottom, we have the service space for a given application domain that consists of the actual service providers, a.k.a., service instances. The integration layer helps resolve the discrepancy of the service schemas and provides a uniformed view of the service space. It can achieve this by applying the existing data integration techniques [40], which are not the focus of this work. The QoWS manager deals with the collection of quality related information from the service instances. The quality data will be used by the query optimizer to make selection from the competing service providers. The service model captures a set of key features of Web services that lay out a foundation for service query specification, processing, and optimization. The service calculus enables users to use declarative service queries to locate Web services, which is more precise and reliable than the keyword based search. The query processor generates SEPs which can be used by the users to invoke services.

The remainder of this chapter is organized as follows. In Section 3.1, we describe a scenario that will be used as a running example through this chapter. In Section 3.2, we present the formal service model. In Section 3.3 and 3.4 we describe the service calculus and the service algebra, respectively. In Section 3.5, we present the implementation of the algebraic operators. In Section 3.6, we propose a QoWS model, which serves as the cost estimation criteria in the QoWS optimization. Based on the model, we propose two optimization algorithms. We present an analytical model in Section 3.7 and conduct experimental studies in Section 3.8.

Q. Yu and A. Bouguettaya, *Foundations for Efficient Web Service Selection*,
DOI 10.1007/978-1-4419-0314-3_3, © Springer Science+Business Media, LLC 2009

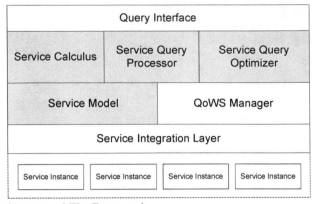

Fig. 3.1 Architecture of The Framework

3.1 Case Study: Car Brokerage

As a way to illustrate this work, we use an application from the *car brokerage* domain (see Figure 3.2). A typical scenario would be of a customer, say Mary, planning to buy a used car having a specific model, make, and mileage. She naturally wants to get the best deal. Assume that Mary has access to a Web service infrastructure where the different entities that play a role in the car purchase are represented by Web services. Examples of Web services that need to be accessed include *Car Purchase (CP), Car Insurance (CI),* and *FInancing (FI)*. A single Web service may provide multiple operations. Different operations may also have dependency relationships. For example, the `paymentHistory` and `financingQuote` operations are both offered by the *financing* service. The latter operation depends on the former operation, i.e., the payment history decides the financing quote. We also anticipate that there will be multiple competitors to provide each of the services mentioned above. It is important that the users' quality requirements be reflected in the service query as criteria for service selection. To purchase an entire car package, Mary would first like to know the price quote of the selected car and the vehicle history report. She then needs to get the insurance quote. Finally, since Mary needs the financing assistance, she also wants to know the financing quote. In addition, Mary may have special requirements on the quality of the service operations. For example, she wants to spend less than 20 dollars to get the vehicle history report.

The proposed service query optimization framework is designed to help Mary with her car package purchase. Mary can specify her car package through a declarative *service query*. The service query is formed based on the service model. The declarative service query is a service calculus expression. It specifies the functionalities that the user wants to retrieve in terms of service operations. There is no need for the user to have the knowledge of the dependency constraints between service operations. In addition, the

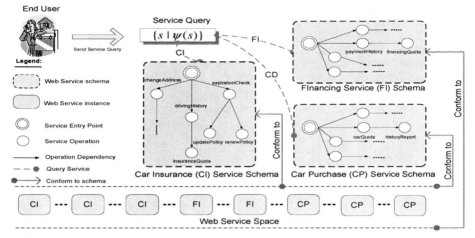

Fig. 3.2 The Car Brokerage Scenario

service query also allows the user to specify the requirements on the quality of the service operations. The service query is then transformed into the *service algebra*, which consists of a set of algebraic operators. The *algebraic optimization* is responsible for achieving the most efficient algebra expression. Service execution plans can then be generated from the retrieved service instances. The *QoWS optimization* is responsible for optimizing the execution plans based on quality.

3.2 Service Query Model

We present our service model in this section. The service model proposes and formally describes two key concepts: *service schema* and *service relation*. The service schema is defined to capture the key features of all Web services across an application domain. It provides a fixed vocabulary and enables the definition of the service query languages. A set of service instances that conform to a service schema form a service relation.

Finite State Machines (FSMs) and Petri-net have previously been proposed to model Web services [12, 41]. However, these models are mainly designed for automating the composition of Web services [67]. Our proposed service model is different from these existing service models by providing foundational support for service query optimization. It is worth to note that the objective of this work is not to define a completely new model. Instead, we are inspired by the standard relational model and make some key extensions to it that enables service users to efficiently access services with their best desired quality. The benefit of presenting such a model is twofold. First, we can use this model to capture the rich semantics of Web services, including functionality, behavior, and quality. These features are of primary interests for users to access services, which also makes them fundamental for specifying service queries. In the proposed two-level service model, the graph-based service schema is used to capture the functionalities of Web services in terms of the operations they offer. It also captures the dependency relationships between the operations, which determine how these operations can be accessed (called behavior of the service). The service relation is used to capture the quality of the service providers. Second, we can leverage the existing technologies developed for the standard relational databases. For example, we can store our service relation in a relational database and use some relational operators to help implement the proposed service algebra (refer to Section 5 for details). In what follows, we first formally define several important concepts about the service schema. We then give the definition of the service relation.

Definition 3.1. (Service Schema) A service schema is defined as a tuple

$$\mathbf{S} = (SG_1, SG_2, ..., SG_n, \mathcal{D}), \text{with}$$
$$SG_i = (V_i, E_i, \epsilon_i), \ i = 1, ..., n$$

is a directed acyclic graph (DAG), called service graph where

- $V_i = \{op_{ij} | 1 \leq j \leq m\}$ represents a set of service operations.
- ϵ_i is the root of the service graph. It represents the entry point, through which all other operations in the service graph can be accessed. ϵ_i can also be regarded as a special service operation, denoted by op_{i0}. A service graph has only one root.
- $E_i = \{e_{ij} | 1 \leq j \leq l\}$, represents the dependencies between two service operations from the same service graph, denoted by $\prec_{ii}$. $e_{ij} = (op, op')$ is an edge, where $op \in V_i, op' \in V_i$, and $op \neq op'$.
- $\mathcal{D} = \{D_{i,j} | 1 \leq i \leq n \land 1 \leq j \leq n \land i \neq j\}$, represents the dependencies between two non-root operations from *different* service graphs, denoted by $\prec_{ij}$. $D_{i,j} = \{e_{i,j}^k | 1 \leq k \leq l\}$ represents the dependencies between two non-root operations from service graph SG_i and SG_j. $e_{i,j}^k = (op, op')$ is an edge, where $op \in V_i$ and $op' \in V_j$.
- $SG' = SG_i \circ SG_j$, the concatenation of two service graphs is formed by coalescing the root of SG_i and SG_j. Furthermore, $V' = \{op | op \in V_i \lor op \in V_j\}$ and $E' = \{e | e \in E_i \lor e \in E_j \lor e \in D_{i,j}\}$. Figure 3.3 shows an example of the concatenation of two service graphs.   ■

The dependency between two service operations is modeled as $op \prec op'$, where $\prec \in \{\prec_{ii}, \prec_{ij}\}$. $\prec_{ii}$ refers to the *intra-service dependency*, which can only be satisfied by invoking the two service operations by the specified order in the service graph. $\prec_{ij}$ refers to the *inter-service dependency*. It should be satisfied when multiple services are accessed. We assume in Definition 3.1 that there is no dependency between the roots of different service graphs. We

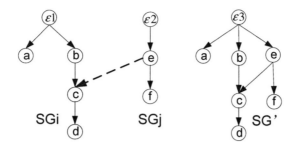

Fig. 3.3 Concatenation of Service Graphs

also assume that multiple dependency constraints on a single operation have an "And" relationship. For example, there are two dependency constraints on op_k, one with op_i and the other with op_j. In this case, both op_i and op_j should be accessed before op_k. It is also worth to note that when there is only one service graph in the service schema **S**, i.e., $n = 1$ in Definition 3.1, **S** becomes a *single-graph* service schema.

Example 3.2. Figure 3.4 shows the service schema for the car brokerage service base. The service schema contains three service graphs, representing the Car Purchase (CP), Car Insurance (CI), and FInancing (FI) services. For example, in CI, there is a set of service operations, such as **drivingHistory** *and* **insuranceQuote**. *These operations collectively represent the functionality of the CI Web service. The dependencies between service operations are captured by the edges in the service graph. For example,* **drivingHistory** *$\prec_{ii}$* **insuranceQuote** *means that the execution of* **insuranceQuote** *depends on the result of* **drivingHistory**. *Service operations from different Web services could have an inter-service dependency. For example, there is a dependency between* **carQuote** *and* **insuranceQuote**. *It is denoted as* **carQuote** *$\prec_{ij}$* **insuranceQuote**. ∎

In what follows, we define a set of key concepts derived from the service schema, including *service path*, *operation graph*, and *operation set graph*. We focus on identifying the important properties they offer that are fundamental to specifying and processing service queries.

Definition 3.3. (Service Path) For a service graph $SG = (V, E, \epsilon)$, we defined a service path $P_i = (\{op_{i1}, ..., op_{ij}, ...op_{ik}\}, E', \epsilon)$ where ϵ is the root of SG, $E' \subseteq E$, and $k \geq 1$; $op_{ij} \in V$ for $1 \leq j \leq k$; and for each $op_{ij}, 0 \leq j \leq (k-1), \exists e_j \in E' : e_j = (op_{ij}, op_{i(j+1)})$ (note that when $j = 0$, op_{ij} becomes ϵ). P_i is an induced subgraph of service graph SG. ∎

Lemma 3.4. *For any service operation $op \in SG$, there must be at least one service path P that can reach op from ϵ.*

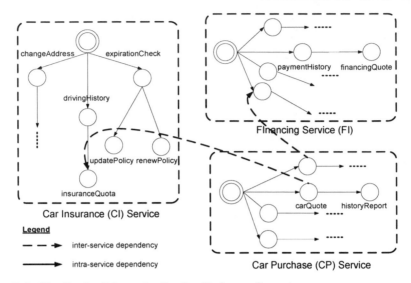

Fig. 3.4 The Service Schema for the Car Brokerage Scenario

PROOF: This directly follows the definition of ϵ. Since ϵ is the entry point to access any other operation (including op) in the service graph, there must be at least one path from it to op.   ∎

Definition 3.5. (Operation Graph) For a service graph $SG = (V, E, \epsilon)$, an operation graph $G(op)$ is the *union* of all the service paths in SG that lead to operation op, $G(op) = \cup Pi$, where $P_i = (\{op_{i1}, ..., op_{ij}, ...op\}, E_i, \epsilon)$. $G(op)$ is an induced subgraph of the service graph SG. Figure 3.5 shows an operation graph $G(d)$, which is formed from SG by the union of two service paths, P_1 and P_2, that both lead to the service operation d.   ∎

Definition 3.6. (Operation Set Graph) For a service graph $SG = (V, E, \epsilon)$, we define an operation set graph $G(\mathbf{op}) = \cup_{i=1}^{k} G(op_i)$, where $\mathbf{op} = \{op_i | 1 \leq i \leq k\}$. $G(\mathbf{op})$ is an induced subgraph of service graph SG. For example, in Figure 3.5, the operation set graph for {a,d,f} is SG itself, i.e., $G(\{a, d, f\}) = SG$.   ∎

Operation graph and operation set graph are central to service query specification and processing. We identify their key properties by using the concepts of *accessible operation* and *accessible graph*. It is worth noting that the root of a service graph is accessible because the root is defined as the entry point of a service. The formal definitions are given as follows.

Definition 3.7. (Accessible Operation) op is an operation in a service graph SG and a general graph G is a subgraph of SG. op is an accessible operation of G if the following two conditions are satisfied:

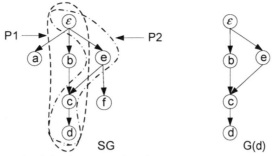

Fig. 3.5   An Example of An Operation Graph

(i) $op \in G$;

(ii) $\forall op'$, $(op', op) \in SG \Rightarrow op'$ is an accessible operation of G.   ∎

Lemma 3.8. *An operation op is an accessible operation of G iff op and all of its preceding nodes in the service graph are included in G.*

PROOF: This directly follows from Definition 3.7.   ∎

Definition 3.9. (Accessible Graph) G is an accessible graph if each operation in G is an accessible operation of G.   ∎

Theorem 3.10. *An operation graph G(op) is a minimal accessible graph for op.*

PROOF: We use two steps to prove this theorem. First, we prove that $G(op)$ is an accessible graph. Second, we prove its minimality.

We can prove $G(op)$ is an accessible graph by proving that op is an accessible operation of $G(op)$. Assume that op is not an accessible operation of $G(op)$. Since $op \in G(op)$, there exists an operation op' where op' is a preceding node of op in SG and op' is not a node of $G(op)$ (Lemma 3.8). Let P_1 be the path from op' to op. From Lemma 3.4, there is a path from ϵ to op', which is denoted by P_2. Connecting P_1 and P_2, we get a new path P_3 from ϵ to op, which is not included in $G(op)$. This contradicts Definition 3.5. Therefore, no such op' exists. We can conclude that $G(op)$ is an accessible graph.

Assume that $G(op)$ is an accessible graph but not minimal for op. Therefore, there exists a graph $G'(op) = G(op) - op'$, where $op' \neq op$, such that $G'(op)$ is still an accessible graph and op is its accessible operation. From Definition 3.5, there is a path to op which passes through op' in SG. Therefore, op' is a preceding node of op in SG. Since op is an accessible operation of $G'(op)$, from Lemma 3.8, we can get $op' \in G'(op)$. This contradicts the fact that op' is removed from $G'(op)$. Therefore, $G(op)$ is a accessible graph and minimal for op.   ∎

Theorem 3.11. *An operation set graph G(**op**) is a minimal accessible graph for **op**.*

PROOF: This directly follows from Definition 3.6 and Theorem 3.10.   ∎

Table 3.1 QoWS Parameters

Parameter	Definition	Domain	Index
Latency	$\text{Time}_{process}(op) + \text{Time}_{results}(op)$ where $\text{Time}_{process}$ is the time to process op and $\text{Time}_{results}$ is the time to transmit/receive the results	number	1
Reliability	$\text{N}_{success}(op)/\text{N}_{invoked}(op)$ where $\text{N}_{success}$ is the number of times that op has been successfully executed and $\text{N}_{invoked}$ is the total number of invocations	number	2
Availability	$\text{UpTime}(op)/\text{TotalTime}(op)$ where UpTime is the time op was accessible during the total measurement time TotalTime	number	3
Fee	Dollar amount to execute the operation	number	4
Reputation	$\sum_{u=1}^{n} Ranking_u(op)/n$, $1 \leq \text{Reputation} \leq 10$ where $Ranking_u$ is the ranking by user u and n is the number of the times op has been ranked	number	5

Remark 3.12. In a service query, users only need to specify the operation(s) they want to access (i.e., in a declarative way). An operation(set) graph will be generated when the query is processed. For example, a user wants financingQuote *and formulates a service query to access it. An operation graph G (financingQuote) will be generated. The query processor will use the operation(set) graph as the single-graph service schema to generate service execution plans (i.e., SEPs). Since an operation(set) graph is an accessible graph, it guarantees that the operations specified in the service query are accessible through the generated SEPs. In addition, the minimality of the graph also guarantees that only minimum number of service operations (i.e., the ones that the operations in the query depends on) are included in the SEPs.∎*

We have now defined the service schema related concepts and identified the key properties they offer for querying service. The service relation defines a set of service instances that conform to the service schema. The service instances offer the operations and follow the dependency constraints defined in the service graphs. However, since the service instances are provided by different service providers, they may have different quality properties. In what follows, we first define a QoWS model to capture the quality features of services. We then give the definition of a service relation.

Definition 3.13. (QoWS Model) The QoWS model formally defines a set of quality parameters for Web services (see Table 3.1). It divides the quality parameters into two categories: *runtime* quality and *business* quality.

- **Runtime quality:** It represents the measurement of properties that are related to the execution of an operation op. We identify three runtime quality parameters: *latency, reliability,* and *availability*. The *latency* measures the expected delay between the moment when op is initiated and the time op sends the results. The *reliability* of op is the ability of the operation to be executed within the maximum expected time frame. The *availability* is the probability that the operation is accessible. Service providers could publish runtime qualities of their Web service operations in the service description or offer mechanisms to query them.

- **Business quality:** It allows the assessment of an operation *op* from a business perspective. We identify two business quality parameters: *fee* and *reputation*. The *fee* gives the dollar amount required to execute *op*. The *reputation* of *op* is a measure of the operation's trustworthiness. It mainly depends on the ratio to which the actual provision of the service is compliant with its promised one. The fee quality can be obtained based on the service providers' advertisement in the service description whereas the reputation is based on the ranking of the end-users.   ■

The values of the parameters defined in the QoWS model are from the number domain, which consists of integer, float, and double. The proposed QoWS model can be extended by adding other quality parameters. The index number given in Table 3.1 will be used by the *labeling function* defined in the service relation.

Definition 3.14. (Service Relation) A service relation SR with a service graph $SG = (V, E, \epsilon)$ is defined as a set of service instances $\mathcal{I} = \{(sid, op_1, ..., op_n)\}$, where

- sid is the unique service id;
- op is a service operation and defined as a pair $op = (opid, \lambda(op))$, where $opid$ is the operation id and λ is a labeling function that assign to each service operation op a set of values to its QoWS parameters, denoted by $\mathbf{Q} = \bigcup_{i=1}^{k} Q_i$. $op \xrightarrow{\lambda} \mathbf{Q}$ gives the quality parameter values for op. $\lambda_i(op) = Q_i$ specifies the ith quality parameter for op, where i is the index for the quality parameter. Table 3.1 specifies the indices for all the QoWS parameters. We will use these indices to refer to the different QoWS parameters in later sections.
- Each service instance $\mathcal{I}$ in SR conforms to the service graph SG, i.e., operations in $\mathcal{I}$ are defined in SG and the operations follow the dependency constraints specified by SG.   ■

We define the domain of $\lambda(op)$ as $dom(\lambda(op)) = \{dom(\lambda_i(op))|1 \leq i \leq m\}$, where m is the number of QoWS parameters that can be applied to op. Therefore, we can further define $dom(op) = \{dom(opid), dom(\lambda_i(op))\}$.

Based on the domain definition, we can restate the above definition of a service relation as follows. A service relation SR is a $(n+1)$-degree relation on the domains of $dom(sid), dom(op_1), dom(op_2), ..., dom(op_n)$, where $op_i \in SG$ for i = 1,...,n,

$$r(SG) \subseteq (dom(sid) \times dom(op_1) \times ... \times dom(op_n))$$

Figure 3.6 shows an example of CI service relation. The service relation contains 5 service instances (a.k.a. service tuples) and has (n+1) fields, which correspond to the *sid* and n service operations offered by the service instances.

The *functionality, behavior*, and *quality* parameters of the Web service are captured in the service model. This provides fundamental support for querying services. Since the functionality of a Web service is offered through a set

Car Insurance (CI)

sid	drivingHistory	insuranceQuote	upldatePolicy	changeAddress	...	OPn
1	{op11,(20,0.8,0.9,25,4)}	{op12,(20,0.6,0.9,8,0,4)}	{op13,(25,0.9,0.8,0,4)}	{op14,(15,0.6,0.9,0,4)}	...	{op1n,(20,0.7,0.9,0,4)}
2	{op21,(30,1.0,0.9,15,3)}	{op22,(30,0.5,0.9,5,3)}	{op23,(50,0.6,0.7,0,3)}	{op24,(30,0.6,0.9,0,3)}	...	{op2n,(15,0.8,0.8,0,4)}
3	{op31,(10,1.0,0.9,30,5)}	{op32,(10,0.9,0.9,10,5)}	{op33,(20,0.8,0.8,0,5)}	{op34,(10,0.9,0.9,0,5)}	...	{op3n,(40,0.8,0.9,0,5)}
4	{op41,(50,0.8,0.9,10,2)}	{op42,(40,0.3,0.4,10,2)}	{op43,(80,0.4,0.5,0,2)}	{op44,(50,0.3,0.5,0,2)}	...	{op4n,(25,0.4,0.7,0,2)}
5	{op51,(15,0.8,0.9,20,3)}	{op52,(30,0.6,0.5,5,3)}	{op53,(30,0.6,0.7,20,3)}	{op54,(20,0.6,0.9,10,3)}	...	{op5n,(45,0.5,0.8,10,3)}

Fig. 3.6 An Example of CI Service Relation

of service operations, the vertices in V collectively represent the functionality of the Web service. The behavior of the service is reflected by the operation graphs (or operation set graph), which contain a set of service operations and the dependency relationship between them. The quality parameters can be attached to the service operations to evaluate QoWS parameters of operations from service instances.

3.3 Service Calculus

We propose a service calculus that enables a declarative specification of service queries. We first give the formal definition of the proposed service calculus. We use our running example to illustrate how the service calculus can help users to get their desired services.

Definition 3.15. (Service Query) A service query is a service calculus expression taking the following form: $\{s \mid \psi(s)\}$, where s is a service tuple variable representing some service instance in a service relation SR. ψ is a formula of the service calculus. Formulas are defined recursively from atoms, which can take one of the following formats:

- $x\ \theta_q\ y$, where (i) θ_q is a QoWS parameter comparison operator taken from $\{=, >, \geq, <, \leq, \neq\}$; (ii) x and y can be QoWS parameters or constants.
- $s.\mathbf{op} == t.\mathbf{op}$, where (i) $s.\mathbf{op}$ denotes the service operations of service tuple s and $t.\mathbf{op}$ denotes the service operations of service tuple t; (ii) $s.\mathbf{op} ==$ $t.\mathbf{op}$ takes a *True* value if s and t have the same (i.e., the signatures are the same) set of service operations whereas it takes a *False* value if otherwise.

- $SR(s)$, where (i) SR is a service relation; (ii) s is a service tuple variable; (iii) $SR(s)$ takes a *True* value if s belongs to SR whereas the atom takes a *False* value if otherwise.   ■

Formulas are defined recursively from atoms using conjunction ($\land$), disjunction ($\lor$), negation ($\neg$), universal quantification ($\forall$), and existential quantification ($\exists$). A variable is *bound* if it is introduced by using ($\forall u$) or ($\exists u$) whereas it is *free* if otherwise. s is the only free variable in ψ. More specifically, formulas are defined in three forms: (i) Every atom is a formula. (ii) $\psi_1 \lor \psi_2$, $\psi_1 \land \psi_2$, and $\neg\psi$ are formulas if ψ_1, ψ_2, and ψ are formulas. (iii) ($\forall s$)(ψ) and ($\exists s$)(ψ) are formulas if ψ_1 and ψ_2 are formulas.

We use two examples to illustrate the usage of service queries.

Example 3.16. Suppose that a user wants to get a vehicle history report with less than 20 dollars. The service query can be expressed as follows:

$$Q_1 = \{s.sid, s[G(historyReport)] | CP(s) \land fee(s.historyReport) \leq 20]\}$$

where,

- $G(historyReport)$ *is an operation graph. Recall that in Theorem 3.10, we proved that an operation graph $G(op)$ is a minimum accessible graph for op. $G(historyReport)$ consists of all the necessary operations that make* historyReport *accessible. It also specifies the dependency constraints for accessing these operations. Therefore, $G(historyReport)$ is the schema (i.e., G_s) for the retrieved service relation.*
- *The [ ] operator in $s[G(historyReport)]$ selects the operations in $G(historyReport)$ from s, including two operations:* carQuote, historyReport.
- $fee(s.historyReport)$ *refers to the fee of the* historyReport *operation in s.*   ∎

Example 3.17. Suppose that the user also wants to get the insurance quote for free. Since vehicle history report and insurance quote are from car purchase service and insurance service respectively, there is a need to compose these two services. The service query can be expressed as follows:

$$Q_2 = \{s.sid, s[G(op_1) \circ G(op_2)] | (\exists s_1)(\exists s_2)(CP(s_1) \land fee(s_1.op_1) \leq 20 \land$$
$$CI(s_2) \land fee(s_2.op_2) = 0 \land s.\mathbf{op} == s_1.\mathbf{op} \circ s_2.\mathbf{op})\}$$

where,

- *s.sid is a new service id for the combined service tuple.*
- $G(op_1) \circ G(op_2)$ *represents graph concatenation (see Definition 3.1 for details), where op_1 and op_2 are* historyReport *and* insuranceQuote *service operations respectively. Similar to Example 3.16, the resultant graph from the concatenation is the schema (i.e., G_s) for the retrieved service relation.*

- $s_1.\mathbf{op} \circ s_2.\mathbf{op}$ *represents service tuple concatenation. If s_1 and s_2 have m and n service operations respectively, the result of service tuple concatenation will be an operation set with $(m+n)$ service operations, with the first m operations from s_1 and the following n operations from s_2.*   ∎

The service calculus enables a service user to formulate a query by specifying the required functionality in terms of service operations. It also allows the user to specify quality requirements on specific operation (e.g., `historyReport` in Example 3.16). The calculus service query retrieves a service relation SR that consists of the service instances satisfying the query predicates. An intermediate service graph, G_s, will also be generated that serves as the schema for the retrieved service instances. G_s is actually an operation (set) graph (e.g., $G(historyReport)$ in Example 3.16) or the concatenation of multiple operation (set) graphs (e.g., $G(op_1) \circ G(op_2)$ in Example 3.17) if a service query needs to access multiple services. The operation (set) comes from the operation(s) that the user wants to access (e.g., `historyReport` in Example 3.16) through the service query.

Remark 3.18. In the above two examples, the service calculus enables a service user to formulate a query by specifying the required functionality in terms of service operations. It also allows the user to specify quality requirements on specific operation (e.g., `historyReport` in Example 3.16). The calculus service query retrieves a service relation that consists of the service instances satisfying the query predicates. An intermediate service graph, G_s, will also be generated that serves as the schema for the retrieved service instances. G_s is actually an operation (set) graph (e.g., $G(historyReport)$ in Example 3.16) or the concatenation of multiple operation (set) graphs (e.g., $G(op_1) \circ G(op_2)$ in Example 3.17) if a service query needs to access multiple services. The operation (set) comes from the operation(s) that the user wants to access (e.g., `historyReport` in Example 3.16) through the service query. ∎

3.4 Service Query Algebra

We define a service query algebra that enables the specification of algebraic service queries. The proposed service algebra contains three major operators that help service users query their desired services:

- **Functional map (F-map):** It facilitates users to locate and invoke their desired functionalities in terms of service operations by making use of the key properties provided by the operation (set) graphs.
- **Quality-based selection (Q-select):** It allows users to locate service instances (i.e., service providers) with their desired quality.
- **Composition (Compose):** It enables service composition when users need to access multiple services.

Service users can use the algebraic operators to access one or multiple services with their desired functionality and quality. A service query is typically specified with the combination of the above three operators (More detailed definition for each of these operators are given in Section 4.1). Querying services is an integrated process that requires to query both the service graphs defined in the service schema and the service relation. Processing an algebraic service query will result in a service relation SR' and a service graph, G_s, that serves as the schema for the retrieved service relation. G_s is constructed based on the operations specified in the service query (i.e., the functionalities a user wants to access). G_s consists of the operations in the service query and all their dependent operations. It also specifies the dependency constraints between these operations. In this section, we first present the service query algebra. We then present a set of algebraic equivalent rules that enable the query optimizer to rewrite the algebraic expressions.

3.4.1 Algebraic Operators

The service algebra consists of three major operators: F-map (χ), Q-select (δ), and Compose ($\oplus$). The algebra operators are applied to a service relation and produce a new service relation.

3.4.1.1 F-map

The F-map operator, denoted by χ, is used to map a service relation SR onto a subset of (user selected) service operations and result in a service relation SR'. The service schema of SR' is a service graph G_s, which is an operation set graph built upon the user specified operations and the service graph of SR. The F-map operator is also called **functional map** because users can choose their desired functionality (in terms of service operations) using this operator. F-map is formally defined as follows:

$$\chi_{\mathbf{op}}(SR) = \{s.sid, s[G(\mathbf{op})] | SR(s)\}$$

where

- **op** is the set of service operations that a user wants to select to achieve the desired functionality.
- $G(\mathbf{op})$ is an operation set graph. It contains the service operations specified by the service query and all their dependent operations. Recall that in Theorem 3.10, we proved that an operation graph is a minimum accessible graph for op. It consists of all the necessary operations that make the operation specified in the service query accessible. It also specifies the dependency constraints for accessing these operations. Therefore, the operation (set) graph can be regarded as the schema (i.e., G_s) for the retrieved service relation.
- The [ ] operator selects the operations from s with respect to $G(\mathbf{op})$, i.e., the retrieved service tuple only contains all the operations of $G(\mathbf{op})$.

Example 3.19. An algebraic service query that retrieves the `insuranceQuote` *operation from the CI service relation is interpreted as follows:*

$$\chi_{\{insuranceQuote\}}(CI) = \{s.sid, s[G(\{insuranceQuote\}]|CI(s)\}$$

∎

3.4.1.2 Q-Select

The `Q-select` operator, denoted by δ, is used to select a subset of service tuples from service relation SR that satisfy some *quality requirement*. The selected tuples form a service relation SR', which has the same service schema as SR. `Q-select` is also called **quality select**. The quality requirement is specified by the *select quality predicate* p_s. `Q-select` is formally defined as follows:

$$\delta_{p_s}(SR) = \{s|SR(s) \wedge p_s(s)\}$$

where

- SR is a general service algebra expression which results in a service relation; $SR(s)$ takes *True* if s belongs to the generated service relation, *False* otherwise.
- p_s is a select quality predicate, which connects a set of *clauses* using the boolean operators: conjunction ($\wedge$), disjunction ($\vee$), and negation ($\neg$). A clause has the form of $x\ \theta_q\ c$ and returns a boolean, where (i) θ_q is a QoWS parameter comparison operator taken from $\{=, >, \geq, <, \leq, \neq\}$; (ii) x is a QoWS parameter and c is a constant.

Example 3.20. An algebraic service query that retrieves the CI service instances with a vehicle history report cost less than 20 dollars can be interpreted as follows:

$$\delta_{\lambda_4(drivingHisotry)\leq 20}(CI) = \{s|CI(s) \wedge \lambda_4(s.drivingHisotry) \leq 20\}$$

The following algebra expression combines the **F-map** *and the* **Q-select** *operators:*

$$\chi_{\{insuranceQuote\}}(\delta_{\lambda_5(insuranceQuote)\geq 3}(CI))$$
$$= \{s.sid, s[G(insuranceQuote)]|CI(s) \wedge \lambda_5(s.insuranceQuote) \geq 3\}$$

∎

3.4.1.3 Compose

The `Compose` operator, denoted by $\oplus$, combines two service relations SR_1 and SR_2 into a single service relation SR'. The service schema of SR' is the concatenation of the service graphs of SR_1 and SR_2, i.e., $G_s = G_1 \circ G_2$. It is used to address the complex service queries that require the cooperation of multiple services. Users can specify their quality requirement over multiple services by using the *compose quality predicate* p_c. These requirements will be used to select service tuples from the combined service relation. Compose is formally defined as follows:

$$SR_1 \oplus_{p_c} SR_2 = \{s.sid, s[G_1 \circ G_2] | (\exists s_1)(\exists s_2)($$
$$SR_1(s_1) \wedge SR_2(s_2) \wedge s.\mathbf{op} == (s_1.\mathbf{op} \circ s_2.\mathbf{op}) \wedge p_c(s))\}$$

where

- G_1 and G_2 are the service graphs of SR_1 and SR_2 respectively. $G_1 \circ G_2$ represents graph concatenation (see Definition 3.1 for details).
- p_c is a *quality predicate*, which connects a set of clauses using the conjunction ($\wedge$) operator. Each clause takes the form of $x \, \theta_q \, y$, where x is a QoWS parameter of a service operation from SR_1 and y is a QoWS parameter of a service operation from SR_2.
- $s.\mathbf{op} == t.\mathbf{op}$ takes a *True* value if s and t have the same set of service operations (i.e., the signatures are the same) whereas it takes a *False* value otherwise, where $s.\mathbf{op}$ denotes the service operations of service tuple s and $t.\mathbf{op}$ denotes the service operations of service tuple t.
- $s_1.\mathbf{op} \circ s_2.\mathbf{op}$ represents service tuple concatenation. If s_1 and s_2 have m and n service operations respectively, the result of service tuple concatenation will be an operation set with $(m + n)$ service operations[1], with the first m operations from s_1 and the following n operations from s_2.

Example 3.21. The following algebraic expression applies to two service relations, CP and CI. It retrieves the combined tuples, in which the insuranceQuote *operation has a higher availability than the* carQuote *operation.*

$$\chi_{\{op_1, op_2\}}(CP \oplus_{\lambda_3(op_1) < \lambda_3(op_2)} CI) = \{s.sid, s[G(op_1) \circ G(op_2)] | (\exists cp)(\exists ci$$
$$(CP(cp) \wedge CI(ci) \wedge s.\mathbf{op} == (cp.\mathbf{op} \circ ci.\mathbf{op}) \wedge \lambda_3(cp.op_1) < \lambda_3(ci.op_2))\}$$

where op_1 and op_2 represent the service operations carQuote *and* insuranceQuote *respectively. The query combines the* Compose *operator and the* F-map *operator. The schema of the resulted service relation SR' is the concatenation of two operation (set) graphs, i.e., $G_s = G(op_1) \circ G(op_2)$.* ∎

If a user does not specify any quality predicate, p_c becomes empty. We define a Compose operator with empty quality predicate as Crossover, denoted as $\otimes$. Crossover is interpreted the same way as Compose by only removing the p_c part.

---

[1] The service schema is designed to have different service graphs with different functionalities (i.e., different set of operations). In this regards, the set of operations for two service graphs are disjoint.

Table 3.2 Algebraic Equivalent Rules

1. Associative rule
$SR_1 \Omega (SR_2 \Omega SR_3) = (SR_1 \Omega SR_2) \Omega SR_3, \ \forall \Omega \in \{\oplus_p, \otimes\}$
$\quad$ if p is applicable to operations from SR_1 and SR_2
2. Communicative rule
$SR_1 \Omega SR_2 = SR_2 \Omega SR_1, \ \forall \Omega \in \{\oplus_p, \otimes\}$
3. Cascading rule
3.1. $\chi_{\mathbf{op_1}}(\chi_{\mathbf{op_2}}(...(\chi_{\mathbf{op_n}}(SR)))) = \chi_{\mathbf{op_1} \cup \mathbf{op_2} ... \cup \mathbf{op_n}}(SR)$
3.2. $\delta_{p_1}(\delta_{p_2}(...(\delta_{p_n}(SR)))) = \delta_{p_1 \wedge p_2 ... \wedge p_n}(SR)$
4. Swapping rule
4.1. $\chi_{\mathbf{op}}(\delta_p(SR)) = \delta_p(\chi_{\mathbf{op}}(SR))$, if operations in p are only from $\mathbf{op}$
4.2. $\chi_{\mathbf{op_1} \cup \mathbf{op_2}}(SR_1 \Omega SR_2) = (\chi_{\mathbf{op_1}}(SR_1)) \Omega (\chi_{\mathbf{op_1}}(SR_2)), \ \forall \Omega \in \{\oplus_p, \otimes\}$
$\quad$ if $\mathbf{op_1}$ and $\mathbf{op_2}$ are the operations from SR_1 and SR_2 respectively
$\quad$ and p is applicable to operations from $\chi_{\mathbf{op_1}}(SR_1)$ and $\chi_{\mathbf{op_2}}(SR_2)$
4.3. $\delta_{p_1 \wedge p_2}(SR_1 \Omega SR_2) = (\delta_{p_1}(SR_1)) \Omega (\delta_{p_2}(SR_2)), \forall \Omega \in \{\oplus_p, \otimes\}$
$\quad$ if operations in p_1 and p_2 are only from SR_1 and SR_2 respectively
4.4. $\Omega_1(SR_1 \Omega_2 SR_2) = (\Omega_1(SR_1)) \Omega_2 (\Omega_1(SR_2)),$
$\quad \forall \Omega_1 \in \{\delta_p, \chi_{\mathbf{op}}\}, \ \forall \Omega_2 \in \{\oplus_p, \otimes\}$

3.4.2 Algebraic Equivalent Rules

We present a set of *algebraic equivalent rules* in this section. Algebraic rewriting can be performed based on these rules. This enables algebraic optimization to generate efficient Service Query Plans (SQPs). Table 3.2 gives the details of each of these algebraic equivalent rules.

The correctness of the algebraic rules can be proved directly from the definition of our service algebra. These rules lay out a foundation for algebraic rewriting. We now present our heuristic rules for finding efficient SQPs. We assume that the internal form of a service query is implemented using a parse tree.

1. Split the `Q-select` with multi-clause predicates into a set of cascading `Q-selects` with single-clause predicates by using cascading rule **3.2.**
2. Move `Q-selects` towards the leaves of the parse tree by using swapping rules, **4.1, 4.3,** and **4.4**
3. Split the `F-map` with multiple sets of operations into a set of cascading `F-maps` with single set of operations by using cascading rule **3.1.**
4. Move `F-maps` towards the leaves of the parse tree by using swapping rules, **4.2, 4.3,** and **4.4.**
5. Combine cascading `Q-selects` and `F-maps` into a single `Q-select`, a single `F-map`, or a `Q-select` followed by a `F-map` by using cascading rules, **3.1, 3.2,** and swapping rule **4.1.**

3.5 Implementing the Algebraic Operators

We present the implementation of the algebraic operators in this section. This enables the generation of SEPs that can be directly used by service users to access services. In relational databases, there is a strong correspondence between algebraic operators and the low-level primitives of the physical system [71]. This correspondence comes from the mapping between relations and files, and tuples and records [78]. In our service query framework, the service execution plan depends on both the service instances and the *shape* of the service graph. The service instances are offered by the actual service providers. The service graph serves as the schema of the service instances. It specifies the dependency constraints of accessing the service operations in the service instances.

3.5.1 Storing the Service Relations

We leverage the relational database approach to store service instances. A service relation can be mapped to a set of database relations and stored in a relational database. Service relations allow *nonatomic* attributes. For example, a service operation is a composite attribute, which consists of an operation id ($opid$) and a set of QoWS values ($\lambda(op)$). This makes a service relation a *nested relation*. Therefore, a service relation contradicts with the First Normal Form (**1NF**) of relational databases. To normalize service relations into 1NF, we need to remove the nested relation attributes into new relations and propagate the primary key into it. A service relation

$$SR(sid, \{op_1(opid, \lambda(op_1))\}, ..., \{op_n(opid, \lambda(op_n))\})$$

is decomposed into $(m + 1)$ database relations:

$$opid(SR)(sid, opid(op_1), ..., opid(op_n)) \tag{1}$$
$$\lambda_1(SR)(sid, \lambda_1(op_1), ..., \lambda_1(op_n)) \tag{2}$$
$$...$$
$$\lambda_m(SR)(sid, \lambda_m(op_1), ..., \lambda_m(op_n)) \tag{$m+1$}$$

Figure 3.7 illustrates the normalization process. SR is a service relation (see Figure 3.7(a)). The op_i attribute is multivalued, which contradicts with 1NF. The normalization decomposes SR into $(m+1)$ 1NF relations, as shown in Figure 3.7(b). Normalization transforms a service relation into a set of database relations. Service relations can thus be stored in relational databases.

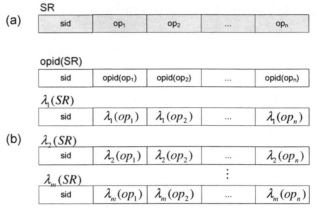

Fig. 3.7 Normalizing service relations into 1NF

3.5.2 Implementing the Service Algebra

New service graphs might need to be generated when processing the algebraic service queries. Generating a new service graph is usually not as straightforward as generating a new relational data schema. Among the three algebraic operators, `F-map` and `Compose` require the generation of new service graphs. Therefore, implementation of these two operators consists of two major tasks: *generating the service graph* and *retrieving service instances*. The `Q-select` operator does not involve any update of the service graph. It only retrieves the service instances based on the quality requirement.

3.5.2.1 F-map

Service Graph Generation: The `F-map` operator employs an algorithm called OSG_{gen} (i.e., Operation-Set-Graph generation) to output an operation set graph given a set of service operations and a service graph. The resultant operation set graph will be the schema for the new service relation generated by the `F-map` operator. Algorithm 1 illustrates the Operation-set-graph generation process.

Service Instance Retrieval: The `F-map` operator performs database projections on each of the quality value relations and the service id relation, i.e., $\Pi_{opid(Gop_1),...,opid(Gop_k)}(opid(SR))$, $\Pi_{\lambda_1(Gop_1),...,\lambda_1(Gop_k)}(\lambda_1(SR))$,..., and $\Pi_{\lambda_m(Gop_1),...,\lambda_m(Gop_k)}(\lambda_m(SR))$, where Gop_1,..., and Gop_k are the operations from service graph G.

3.5.2.2 Q-select

Service Instance Retrieval: The Q-select operator uses five steps to retrieve service instances:

1. Divide the selection predicate $p(\lambda_1, \lambda_2..., \lambda_k)$ into k subpredicates $p(\lambda_1)$, $p(\lambda_2)...,p(\lambda_k)$, where k is the number of distinct quality parameters in the selection predicate.
2. Use the subpredicates to perform database selection, $\sigma_{p(\lambda_1)}(\lambda_1(SR))$, $\sigma_{p(\lambda_2)}(\lambda_2(SR))...$, and $\sigma_{p(\lambda_k)}(\lambda_k(SR))$.
3. Perform database projection on the resultant relations from step 2 to retrieve the service id, $sid_{\lambda_1} = \Pi_{sid}(\sigma_{p(\lambda_1)}(\lambda_1(SR)))$, $sid_{\lambda_2} = \Pi_{sid}(\sigma_{p(\lambda_2)}(\lambda_2(SR)))$,..., and $sid_{\lambda_k} = \Pi_{sid}(\sigma_{p(\lambda_k)}(\lambda_k(SR)))$.
4. Combine sid_{λ_1}, sid_{λ_2}, ..., sid_{λ_k} to generate the relation SID, which contains all the sids to be retrieved. The combination process is performed based on the boolean operators used to connect different quality parameter clauses in $p(\lambda_1, \lambda_2..., \lambda_k)$. The boolean operator can take one of the following two forms: $\vee$ and $\wedge$. For example, if $p = c(\lambda_1) \wedge c(\lambda_2)$, $SID = sid_{\lambda_1} \cap sid_{\lambda_2}$; if $p = c(\lambda_1) \vee c(\lambda_2)$, $SID = sid_{\lambda_1} \cup sid_{\lambda_2}$
5. Perform database natural join, $opid(SR) \infty SID$, $\lambda_1(SR) \infty SID$,..., and $\lambda_k(SR) \infty SID$ to retrieve the operation id and quality values for the retrieved service instances.

3.5.2.3 Compose

Service Graph Generation: The Compose operator employs an algorithm called G_{con} (i.e., Graph concatenation) to output a new service graph given two service graphs and a set of edges representing inter-service dependencies. The resultant service graph will be the schema for the new service relation generated by the Compose operator. Algorithm 2 illustrates the graph concatenation process.

Service Instance Retrieval: The Compose operator uses five steps to retrieve service instances:

1. Divide the selection predicate p into a set of subpredicates, each of which contains a single clause.
2. Perform database θ-join, $\lambda_i(SR_1) \bowtie_{p(\lambda_i, \lambda_j)} \lambda_j(SR_2)$, where $p(\lambda_i, \lambda_j)$ is a subpredicate containing λ_i and λ_j and λ_i. λ_j can refer to the same quality parameter, for example, $p = \lambda_3(carQuote) < \lambda_3(insureanceQuote)$.
3. Perform database projection on the resultant relations from step 2 to retrieve the service id, $sid_{\lambda_{i,j}} = \Pi_{sid_i, sid_j}(\lambda_i(SR_1) \bowtie_{p(\lambda_i, \lambda_j)} \lambda_j(SR_2))$.
4. Combine $sid_{\lambda_i, \lambda_j}$ to generate the relation SID, which contains all the sids to be retrieved. The combination process is similar to step 4 of the Q-select operator.

5. Perform database natural join, $(opid(SR_1)\infty SID)\infty(opid(SR_2)$, $(\lambda_1(SR_1)\infty SID)\infty\lambda_1(SR_2),...,$ and $(\lambda_k(SR_1)\infty SID)\infty\lambda_k(SR_2)$ to retrieve the operation id and quality values for the retrieved service instances.

Algorithm 1 Operation Set Graph Generation (OSG_{con})

Require: A set of service operations **op**=$\{op_1,...,op_n\}$, a service graph SG
Ensure: An operation set graph OSG
 1: $OSG = \phi$;
 2: **for all** $op \in$ **op do**
 3:    $OG = OG_{gen}(SG,op)$;
 4:    $OSG{=}OSG \cup OG$;
 5: **end for**
 6: **Function** $OG_{gen}(SG,op)$
 7: $OG.E{=}\phi$, $OG.V{=}\phi$;
 8: $OG.V = OG.V \cup \{op\}$;
 9: **for all** $e \in SG.E$ **do**
10:    **if** $e.to == op$ **then**
11:      $OG.E = OG.E \cup \{e\}$;
12:      $op' = e.\text{from}$;
13:    **end if**
14: **end for**
15: $OG' = OG_{gen}(OG,op')$;
16: $OG = OG \cup OG'$;

Algorithm 2 Service Graph Concatenation Algorithm (G_{con})

Require: Two service graphs SG_1, SG_2, an edge set $E_D{=}\{e_1,e_2,...,e_n\}$
Ensure: A service graph SG
 1: $SG.V = \phi$, $SG.E = \phi$;
 2: $SG.V = SG_1.V \cup SG_2.V$;
 3: $SG.E = SG_1.E \cup SG_2.E \cup E_D$;
 4: $SG{=}SG{-}\{SG_1.\epsilon, SG_2.\epsilon\}$;
 5: $SG.\epsilon = \epsilon_0$;
 6: **for all** $op \in SG.V$ **do**
 7:    **if** op does not have any incoming edge **then**
 8:      $e' = \{\epsilon, op\}$;
 9:      $SG.E = SG.E \cup \{e'\}$;
10:    **end if**
11: **end for**

3.5.3 Complexity of Service Algebraic Operators

We analyze the complexity of the service algebraic operators in this section. The complexity is defined with respect to the cardinalities of the service relations that are independent of the physical implementation details. We assume the cardinality of the original service relations is t. Table 3.3 summarizes the complexity of each service algebraic operator.

F-map – The `F-map` operator first generates a new service graph by applying OSG_{gen} that has a complexity of $O(n \times (V+E))$. It then retrieves the service instances by performing projection on each relation, include the operation id relation and the m quality value relation. This requires a complexity of $O(m \times t)$. Therefore, the overall complexity is $O(n \times (V + E) + m \times t)$.

Q-select – The `Q-select` operator uses five major steps for retrieving service instances. We analyze the complexity of each step and derive the total complexity in the end.

1. Step 1 divides a complex selection predicate into k subpredicates. It requires one pass of the k subpredicates and has a complexity of $O(k)$.
2. Step 2 performs selection using the k subpredicates on k quality value relations respectively. The complexity is $O(k \times t)$.
3. Step 3 projects the resultant quality value relation onto the *sid* attribute. We assume that the average selection factor in Step 2 is s_F. Therefore, the complexity of step 3 is $O(k \times t \times s_F)$.
4. Step 4 uses the set operators (i.e., $\cap$ and $\cup$) to get the final sids. To eliminate duplicates, we assume that the set operators usually need to sort the relations on the sids and then compare the sids from both relations. Therefore, the complexity is $O((k-1) \times t \times s_F \times log\,(t \times s_F))$.
5. Step 5 joins the final sids with the operation id relation and all the m quality value relation. We assume that natural join also needs to sort the relations on sids. Therefore, the complexity is $O(m \times t \times log\,t)$.

We can derive the overall complexity of the `Q-select` operator as:

$$O(k + k \times t + k \times t \times s_F + (k-1) \times t \times s_F \times log\,t \times s_F + m \times t \times log\,t)$$
$$= O((k+m) \times t \times s_F \times log\,t)$$

Compose – The `Compose` operator first applies the G_{con} to generate a new service graph that requires a complexity of $O(V + E)$. It then uses five major steps for retrieving service instances. We analyze the complexity of each step and derive the overall complexity in the end.

1. Step 1 divides a complex project predicate into k subpredicates. It requires one pass of the k subpredicates and has a complexity of $O(k)$.
2. Step 2 performs θ-join using the k subpredicates respectively. The complexity is $O(k \times t \times log\,t)$.
3. Step 3 projects the resultant quality value relation onto the *sid* attribute. We assume that the average selection factor in Step 2 is s'_F. Therefore, the complexity of step 3 is $O(k \times t^2 \times s'_F)$.
4. Step 4 uses the set operators (i.e., $\cap$ and $\cup$) to get the final sids. To eliminate duplicates, we assume that the set operators usually need to sort

Table 3.3 Complexity of Service Algebraic Operators

Algebraic operator	Complexity
F-map	$O(n \times (V + E) + m \times t)$
Q-select	$O((k + m) \times t \times s_F \times log \ t)$
Compose	$O((V + E) + (k \times t + m) \times t \times log \ t)$
Crossover	$O((V + E) + (m + 1) \times t^2)$

the relations on the sids and then compare the sids from both relations. Therefore, the complexity is $O((k - 1) \times t^2 \times s'_F \times log \ (t^2 \times s'_F))$.

5. Step 5 performs $(opid(SR_1)\infty SID)\infty(opid(SR_2),$ $(\lambda_1(SR_1)\infty SID)\infty\lambda_1(SR_2),...,$ and $(\lambda_m(SR_1)\infty SID)\infty\lambda_k(SR_2)$ to retrieve the operation id and quality values for the retrieved service instances. Since SID has been sorted in Step 4, the complexity is $O(m \times t \times log \ t)$.

We can derive the overall complexity of the Compose operator as:

$$O((V + E) + k + k \times t \times log \ t + k \times t^2 \times s'_F + (k - 1) \times t^2 \times s'_F$$
$$\times log \ (t^2 \times s'_F) + m \times t \times log \ t)$$
$$= O((V + E) + (k \times t + m) \times t \times s'_F \times log \ t)$$

Crossover – The Crossover first applies the G_{con} to generate a new service graph that requires a complexity of $O(V + E)$. It then applies to the operation id relation and the m quality value relation. Therefore, they have a complexity of $O((V + E) + (m + 1) \times t^2)$.

3.5.4 Generating SEPs

The retrieved service relation conforms to the service graphs that define the service operations and their dependency constraints for the service instances in the retrieved service relation. We investigate in this section how to generate SEPs from the retrieved service instances based on the service graphs. The service graphs could be generated during query processing (e.g., if F-map and Compose are involved) or originally defined by the service schema. We propose an algorithm that generates a *service execution path* from a service graph. The service execution path arranges all operations in the service graph into a sequence with respect to all the dependency constraints. A service execution path is non-executable because operations in the path are at the schema level, i.e., these operations are not from any particular service instances. SEPs can be generated by instantiating the service execution path with the operations from the service instances. A SEP is executable in that it is formed by the operations from service instances that correspond to the actual service providers.

Remark 3.22. A Service Execution Plan (SEP) is different from a Service Query Plan (SQP) from two major aspects:

1. *A SEP consists of a set of service operations from the retrieved service instances. A SQP, on the other hand, is composed of algebraic operators and service relations. It is used for retrieving service instances.*

2. *A SEP specifies the order to execute the service operations. A SQP, on the other hand, specifies the order of the algebraic operators and service relations for retrieving service instances.*   ∎

Algorithm 3 Service Execution Path Generation

Require: A Service Graph G
Ensure: A Service Execution Path $P = (\epsilon, op_1, ..., op_n)$
  1: **for all** $op \in G$ **do**
  2:     op.order=-1;
  3: **end for**
  4: **for all** $e \in G$ **do**
  5:     e.color=red;
  6: **end for**
  7: current_order=0;
  8: P[current_order]=ϵ;
  9: ϵ.order=current_order+1;
 10: current_order=current_order+1;
 11: **for all** ϵ's outgoing edge e **do**
 12:     e.color=green;
 13: **end for**
 14: **for all** ϵ's next operation op **do**
 15:     Depth_First_Traversal(G, op, P, current_order);
 16: **end for**
 17: **for all** operation op' **do**
 18:     **if** op'.order==-1 **then**
 19:         Depth_First_Traversal(G, op', P,current_order);
 20:     **end if**
 21: **end for**

Algorithm 4 Depth_First_Traversal

Require: $G, op, P, order$
 1: executable=true;
 2: **for all** op's incoming edge e **do**
 3:     **if** e.color==red **then**
 4:         executable=false;
 5:         break;
 6:     **end if**
 7: **end for**
 8: **if** executable==false **then**
 9:     return;
10: **end if**
11: P[current_order]=op;
12: op.order=current_order+1;
13: current_order=current_order+1;
14: **for all** op's outgoing edge e **do**
15:     e.color=green;
16: **end for**
17: **for all** op's next operation op' **do**
18:     Depth_First_Traversal(G, op', P, current_order);
19: **end for**

Algorithm 3 illustrates the algorithm of generating a service execution path from a service graph. The produced service execution path is an ordered list of service operations. This algorithm has two major features: *edge coloring* and *depth-first traversal*. First, the orders among operations need to conform to the dependency constraints. Therefore, an operation can be executed only after all of its depending operations have been executed. To fulfill this requirement, we color the edges of the graph as green and red. An edge is initially colored as red (line 4-6). Once a service operation is visited, all of its outgoing edges are colored as green (line 11-13). Only the operations with all green incoming edges will be visited. Edge coloring guarantees that service operations can be executed in the order that conforms to dependencies. Second, we use the recursive call to achieve a graph depth-first traversal (shown in Algorithm 4). The graph depth-first traversal will put service operations that come from the same service paths (e.g., `paymentHistory` and `financingQuote`) close to one another in the service execution path. This enables users to continuously perform a set of related operations.

Theorem 3.23. *The execution path generation algorithm has the complexity of $\mathcal{O}|V + E|$.*

PROOF: This algorithm is a graph depth-first traversal algorithm. Therefore, it has the complexity of $\mathcal{O}|V + E|$.   ∎

3.6 Service Query Optimization

The retrieved service relation usually contains more than one service instances. Therefore, multiple SEPs can be generated from the service relation. All these SEPs satisfy the functional and quality requirement specified by the query. However, users may have special preference for some QoWS parameters over others. For example, Mary wants to use the SEP with the highest reputation, i.e., she prefers to buy the car package from the most reputable providers. The preference is on the *entire* SEP that usually contains multiple operations. It is different from the quality requirement in the service query that is on some *individual* operations (e.g., get the history report for less than 20 dollars). The QoWS aware query optimization is a "user centered" optimization. It is to find the SEP with the best quality based on user preference over the entire SEP. In this regard, the service query optimization performs a *global selection* as opposed to *local search* that is performed by the query processor. In this section, we first present a set of aggregation functions to compute the QoWS for SEPs. They combine the QoWS parameters from multiple service operations. An score function is then presented to evaluate the entire SEPs. Finally, we present two optimization algorithms to find the best SEPs.

3.6.1 QoWS for SEPs

We need now to compute the $QoWS$ parameters for the entire service execution plan that may contain multiple service operations. Based on the meaning of $QoWS$, we define a set of aggregation functions to compute $QoWS$ of service execution plans, as shown in Table 3.4. The quality of a SEP can thus be characterized as a vector of QoWS,

$$Quality(SEP_i) = (lat(SEP_i), rel(SEP_i), av(SEP_i), fee(SEP_i), rep(SEP_i)).$$

lat (latency) and fee (usage fee) take scalar values ($\Re^+$). av (availability), and rel (reliability) represent probability values (a real value between 0 and 1). Finally, rep (reputation) ranges over the interval [0,5].

3.6.2 Score Function

We define a score function to compute a scalar value out of the QoWS vector of the SEPs. This can facilitate the comparison of the quality of the SEPs. Since users may have preferences over how their queries are answered, they may specify the relative importance of $QoWS$ parameters. We assign *weights*,

Table 3.4 QoWS for a Service Execution Plan

QoWS parameter	Aggregation function
Latency	$\sum_{i=1}^{n} latency(op_i)$
Reliability	$\prod_{i=1}^{n} rel(op_i)$
Availability	$\prod_{i=1}^{n} av(op_i)$
Fee	$\sum_{i=1}^{n} fee(op_i)$
Reputation	$\frac{1}{n}\sum_{i=1}^{n} rep(op_i)$

ranging from 0 to 1, to each $QoWS$ parameter to reflect the level of importance. Default values are otherwise used.

We use the following score function F to evaluate the quality of the service execution plans. By using the score function, the QoWS optimization is to find the execution plan with the maximum score.

$$F = (\sum_{Q_i \in Neg} W_i \frac{Q_i^{max} - Q_i}{Q_i^{max} - Q_i^{min}} + \sum_{Q_i \in Pos} W_i \frac{Q_i - Q_i^{min}}{Q_i^{max} - Q_i^{min}})$$

where Neg and Pos are the sets of negative and positive $QoWS$ respectively. In negative (resp. positive) parameters, the higher (resp. lower) the value, the worse is the quality. W_i are weights assigned by users to each parameter. Q_i is the value of the ith $QoWS$ of the service execution plan obtained through the aggregate functions from Table 3.4. Q_i^{max} is the maximum value for the ith $QoWS$ parameter for all potential service execution plans and Q_i^{min} is the minimum. These two values can be computed by considering the operations from service instances with the highest and lowest values for the ith $QoWS$.

3.6.3 Optimization Algorithms

The algebraic optimization depends on the "predicate pushdown" rules to perform **Compose** and **Crossover** as late as possible. Since the service algebraic rules also include associative and communicative rules for **Compose** and **Crossover**, many equivalent expressions can still be produced after the algebraic optimization. As the number of **Compose** or **Crossover** in a service query increases, the number of different composition orders may grow rapidly. The objective of service query optimization is to select the most efficient composition order to form a fast SQP. It then selects the SEP with the best user desired quality from the multiple candidates resulted from the SQP.

Algorithm 5 DP Plan Optimization

1: **for all** $i \in [1, k]$ **do**
2:     find the best query plan bestSQP($\{SR_i\}$) for SR_i;
3: **end for**
4: **for all** $i \in [2, k]$ **do**
5:     **for all** $\mathcal{PR} \subseteq \{SR_1, ..., SR_k\}$ s.t. $\|\mathcal{PR}\| = i$ **do**
6:         $\{\mathcal{PR}$ is a set with i service relations$\}$
7:         bestSQP = a system generated SQP with $+\infty$ cost;
8:         **for all** pair $\mathcal{PR}_j, SR_j$ s.t. $\mathcal{PR} = \{SR_j\} \cup \mathcal{PR}_j$ and $SR_j \notin \mathcal{PR}_j$ **do**
9:             $\{\mathcal{PR}_j$ is a set with $(i - 1)$ service relations$\}$
10:             tempSQP = composePlan(bestSQP($\mathcal{PR}_j$), SR_j);
11:             **if** tempSQP.cost < bestSQP.cost **then**
12:                 bestSQP = tempSQP;
13:             **end if**
14:         **end for**
15:         bestSQP($\mathcal{PR}$) = bestSQP;
16:     **end for**
17: **end for**
18: $\{SEP_1, ..., SEP_m\}$ = execute(bestSQP($\{SR_1, ..., SR_k\}$));
19: bestSEP = a system generated SEP with $-\infty$ score;
20: **for all** $i \in [1, m]$ **do**
21:     SEP_i.score = F(SEP_i);
22:     **if** SEP_i.score < bestSEP.score **then**
23:         bestSEP = SEP_i;
24:     **end if**
25: **end for**
26: **return** bestSEP;

Join ordering optimization has been intensively investigated in database research [24, 71]. One of the most adopted approaches is the System-R bottom-up dynamic programming query optimization [71]. A straightforward solution for our service query optimization is to extend the DP optimization approach. Figure 5 shows the extended DP based plan optimization algorithm. It consists of two major phases. The first phase depends on dynamic programming to select the most efficient query plan (line 1-17). The query plan is then executed in the second phase (line 18), which results in a set of SEPs. The second phase then proceeds to select the SEP with the best quality (i.e., the maximum score) (line 19-26). It is worth noting that multiple query plans may coexist even if they share the same join order in the first phase of the algorithm. This is because some query plan may place the service tuples in *interesting orders* that can be beneficial to subsequent algebraic operators [71].

DP optimization performs all Crossovers as late in the join sequence as possible [71]. This implies that in composing service relations $SR_1, SR_2, ..., SR_n$ only those orderings $SR_{i1}, SR_{i2}, ..., SR_{in}$ are examined in which for all j, where $j = 2, ..., n$, either

1. SR_{ij} has at least one join predicate with some relation SR_{ik}, where $k < j$, or

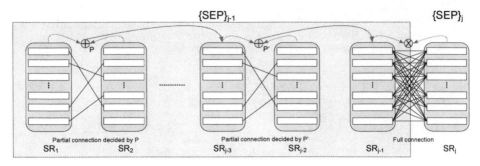

Fig. 3.8   Properties of Crossover

2. $\forall k > j$, SR_{ik} has no compose quality predicate with SR_{i1}, ..., $SR_{i(j-1)}$

All query plans that satisfy the above composition ordering requirement can generate relatively smaller number of intermediate results than other query plans. Therefore, they can be performed more efficiently to generate the SEPs. Since service query optimization aims to select the best SEP, it will be necessary if a query plan can return a subset of the SEPs where the optimal solution is in it. This can effectively reduce the enumeration space. Therefore, we can further improve the DP optimization. The challenge is how to ensure that the optimal solution is included in the subset of SEPs. This is addressed by a special treatment on the Crossover operator.

A Divide-And-Conquer Query Optimization Strategy

Crossover is an expensive algebraic operator. The number of service tuples returned is exponential to the number of service relations that are involved. In this section, we propose an approach to deal with the Crossover operator. This approach enables the optimization process to consider only a small subset of the service execution plans. It guarantees that the subset encompasses the (semi) optimal solution. This greatly improves the system performance while preserving the quality of the selected SEP.

We first investigate some important properties of the Crossover operator. Figure 3.8 helps illustrate these properties. Service relation SR_{j-1} is the result of a sequence of compositions. The service relations (e.g., SR_1 and SR_2) under the Compose operator are "partially connected" based on the compose quality predicate. By "partially connected", we mean that only a subset of service tuples from SR_1 and SR_2 are selected and combined to form the composed relation (see the connections between SR_1 and SR_2 in Figure 3.8). The number of service generated is $card(SR_1) \times card(SR_2) \times SF_J(SR_1, SR_2, p)$, where $SF_J(SR_1, SR_2, p)$ is the *join selectivity factor*. The selectivity factor depends on service relations and the compose quality predicate. It takes a real value between 0 and 1. After the sequence of compositions are performed, service relation SR_{j-1} is combined with SR_j to generate the final result using the `Crossover` operator. Since there is no compose predicate, SR_{j-1} is "fully connected" with SR_j to perform the `Crossover` (see the connections between SR_{j-1} and SR_j in Figure 3.8). This results in $card(SR_{j-1}) \times card(SR_j)$ service tuples. The searching space would be greatly increased by the `Crossover` operator.

We adopt a *divide-and-conquer* strategy to deal with `Crossover`. The strategy generates a set of (sub) optimal *partial SEPs* through local search. It then combines these partial SEPs to form the final SEP. Before going into the details, we first introduce some approximation functions which will be used in this strategy. Two aggregation functions (i.e., the functions for reliability and availability) presented in Table 3.4 do not combine QoWS parameters from multiple service operations in a linear manner. We propose two linear functions to approximate the original functions for aggregation purpose. Specifically,

$$Reliability = \sum_{i=1}^{n} log(rel(op_i)), \quad Availability = \sum_{i=1}^{n} log(av(op_i))$$

These enable to express the score of the final SEP as a linear combination of the scores from the partial SEPs. In the example shown in Figure 3.8, the score of the final SEP is the sum of those from its partial SEPs, i.e., $score(SEP_{ik}) = score(SEP_i^{j-1}) + score(SEP_k^j)$.

SR_{j-1} is fully connected with SR_j through the `Crossover` operator. There must be a connection between the best partial plan in $\{SEP\}_{j-1}$ and the best partial plan in $\{SEP\}_j$. The aggregation of these two partial plans forms the best service execution plan. This is because $best(\{SEP\}).score = best(\{SEP\}_{j-1}).score + best(\{SEP\}_j).score$. Therefore, the optimization algorithm can perform the sequence of joins and query a single (or a set of) service relation(s) separately. This enables to achieve the (semi) final optimal solution through a set of local search without the need to really perform the `Crossover`. We call this optimization strategy the *Divide-And-Conquer-DP (DAC-DP) optimization*. The best partial SEPs can finally be combined to form the (semi) optimal solution. For the case shown in Figure 3.8, only $(card(SR_{j-1}) + card(SR_j))$ service tuples are returned instead of $(card(SR_{j-1}) \times card(SR_j))$. Figure 6 shows the DAC-DP service query optimization algorithm. The algorithm first perform the sequence of compositions on the first t service relations and generate m partial SEPs (line 18). It then selects the best partial SEP (line 20-25). The algorithm then proceeds to query each of the remaining service relations that need to be combined using the `Crossover` operator. It selects the best partial SEP from the query result of each service relation (line 27-34). All the best partial SEPs are then combined to form the final SEP (line 35).

Algorithm 6 DAC-DP Plan Optimization

1: **for all** $i \in [1, k]$ **do**
2:     find the best query plan bestSQP($\{SR_i\}$) for SR_i;
3: **end for**
4: **for all** $i \in [2, k]$ **do**
5:     **for all** $\mathcal{PR} \subseteq \{SR_1, ..., SR_k\}$ s.t. $||\mathcal{PR}|| = i$ **do**
6:         $\{\mathcal{PR}$ is a set with i service relations$\}$
7:         bestSQP = a system generated SQP with $+\infty$ cost;
8:         **for all** pair $\mathcal{PR}_j, SR_j$ s.t. $\mathcal{PR} = \{SR_j\} \cup \mathcal{PR}_j$ and $SR_j \notin \mathcal{PR}_j$ **do**
9:             $\{\mathcal{PR}_j$ is a set with $(i - 1)$ service relations$\}$
10:            tempSQP = composePlan(bestSQP($\mathcal{PR}_j$), SR_j);
11:            **if** tempSQP.cost < bestSQP.cost **then**
12:                bestSQP = tempSQP;
13:            **end if**
14:        **end for**
15:        bestSQP($\mathcal{PR}$) = bestSQP;
16:    **end for**
17: **end for**
18: $\{SEP_1, ..., SEP_m\}$ = execute(bestSQP($\{SR_1, ..., SR_t\}$));
19: bestSEP = a system generated SEP with $-\infty$ score;
20: **for all** $i \in [1, m]$ **do**
21:     SEP_i.score = F(SEP_i);
22:     **if** SEP_i.score < bestSEP.score **then**
23:         bestSEP = SEP_i;
24:     **end if**
25: **end for**
26: **for all** $i \in [(t + 1), k]$ **do**
27:     $\{SEP_1^i, ..., SEP_{m^i}^i\}$ = execute(bestSQP(SR_i));
28:     bestSEP$_i$ = a system generated SEP with $-\infty$ score;
29:     **for all** $j \in [1, m^i]$ **do**
30:         SEP_j^i.score = F(SEP_j^i);
31:         **if** SEP_j^i.score < bestSEP$_i$.score **then**
32:             bestSEP$_i$ = SEP_j^i;
33:         **end if**
34:     **end for**
35:     bestSEP = bestSEP $\otimes$ bestSEP$_i$;
36: **end for**
37: **return** bestSEP;

3.7 Analytical Model

In this section, we present the analytical model for the above optimization algorithms. We analyze the complexity of the DP-based optimization algorithm and the DAC-DP algorithm. Table 3.5 defines the parameters and the symbols used in this section.

Table 3.5 Symbols and Parameters

Variables	Definition
N_{SR}	Total number of service relations
N_{SR}^J	Number of service relations under join
N_{SR}^C	Number of service relations under Cartesian product
N_{IO}	Total number of interesting orders
N_{SI}^i	Number of service instances in the ith service relation
$SF_J(SR_i, SR_{i+1})$	Join selectivity factor between SR_i, SR_{i+1}

3.7.1 DP-based Query Optimization

We start by studying the complexity of the DP-based optimization algorithm. There are two major phases in this algorithm. The first phase is to select the most efficient query plan whereas the second phase is to generate the best service execution plan. In the first phase, the DP optimization algorithm uses two heuristics to reduce the enumeration space. First, it eliminates the permutations that involve Cartesian products. Second, the commutatively equivalent strategies with the highest cost are also eliminated. Therefore, these heuristics help reduce the size of the enumeration space from $N_{SR}!$ to $2^{N_{SR}}$. The algorithm also considers interesting orders, hence the complexity of the first phase is:

$$O(2^{N_{SR}} \times N_{IO}) \tag{3.1}$$

The second phase enumerates the space of SEPs. The size of the SEP space is determined by the number of service relations, number of service instances per service relation, and the join selectivity factor. The join selectivity factor for Cartesian products takes the value of 1 whereas the selectivity factor for the normal join operators takes a value between 0 and 1. The complexity of the second phase is:

$$O(\prod_{i=1}^{N_{SR}} N_{SI}^i \times \prod_{i=1}^{N_{SR}-1} SF_J(SR_i, SR_{i+1})) \tag{3.2}$$

Therefore, the complexity of the entire DP-based optimization algorithm is:

$$O(2^{N_{SR}} \times N_{IO} + \prod_{i=1}^{N_{SR}} N_{SI}^i \times \prod_{i=1}^{N_{SR}-1} SF_J(SR_i, SR_{i+1})) \tag{3.3}$$

3.7.2 DAC-DP Query Optimization

The DAC-DP optimization algorithm consists of two similar phases as the DP-based optimization algorithm. It relies on the divide-and-conquer strategy to reduce the enumeration space in both phases. We assume that there are

Table 3.6 Parameter Settings

Parameters	CP		CI		FI	
	op1	op2	op3	op4	op5	op6
latency	0-300(s)		0-300(s)		0-300(s)	
reliability	0.5-1.0		0.5-1.0		0.5-1.0	
availability	0.7-1.0		0.7-1.0		0.7-1.0	
fee	0-30($)		0-30($)		0-30($)	
reputation	0-5		0-5		0-5	

N_{SR}^J service relations to be combined using join. Therefore, the complexity of the first phase is:

$$O(2^{N_{SR}^J} \times N_{IO}) \tag{3.4}$$

The second phase selects a set of best partial SEPs and then combines them to form the final optimal SEP. Based on our analysis in Section 3.6.3, we can derive the complexity of the second phase is:

$$O(\prod_{i=1}^{N_{SR}^J} N_{SI}^i \times \prod_{i=1}^{N_{SR}^J-1} SF_J(SR_i, SR_{i+1}) + \sum_{i=N_{SR}^J+1}^{N_{SR}} N_{SI}^i) \tag{3.5}$$

Therefore, the complexity of the entire DAC-DP optimization algorithm is:

$$O(2^{N_{SR}^J} \times N_{IO} + \prod_{i=1}^{N_{SR}^J} N_{SI}^i \times \prod_{i=1}^{N_{SR}^J-1} SF_J(SR_i, SR_{i+1}) + \sum_{i=N_{SR}^J+1}^{N_{SR}} N_{SI}^i) \tag{3.6}$$

3.8 Experimental Study

We conducted a set of experiments to assess the performance of the proposed approach. We use the car brokerage scenario as our testing environment to setup the experiment parameters. The purpose is to demonstrate how our approach can help Mary select the best deal. The Web services are developed on Systinet WASP Server, which is a complete platform for development, deployment, and management of Web service based applications [79]. We run our experiments on a cluster of *Sun Enterprise Ultra 10* workstations under *Solaris* operating system.

We create a service schema containing three services, which is similar to the one shown in Figure 3.4. For simplicity, we omit the unnecessary service operations. Each service contains two operations: CP (careQuote, historyReport), CI (drivingHistory, insuranceQuote), and FI (paymentHistory, financingQuote). We create three service relations, which conform to the service schema. The number of service instances in each service relation varies from

10 to 60. We use five QoWS parameters to evaluate service operations: latency, reliability, availability, fee, and reputation. The values of these parameters are generated within a range based on uniform distribution. The user's role is to give the weights for these parameters. Table 5.2 summarizes the potential values for the QoWS parameters for each service operation, where $op_1, op_2, op_3, op_4, op_5, op_6$ represent service operations carQuote, historyReport, paymentHistory, financingQuote, drivingHistory, and insuranceQuote, respectively.

We consider a service query that helps Mary get an entire car package, including the price quote and history report of a used car, insurance quote, and financing quote. The service query can be expressed as a service algebraic expression as follows:

$$Q : \chi_{\{op_1, op_2, op_3, op_4\}} [\delta_{\lambda_4(op_2) \leq 20}(CP) \oplus_{\lambda_3(op_1) < \lambda_3(op_4)} \delta_{\lambda_4(op_3) \leq 20}(CI) \otimes FI]$$
(3.7)

where op_1, op_2, op_6, op_4 represent service operations carQuote, historyReport, insuranceQuote, and fincancingQuote respectively.

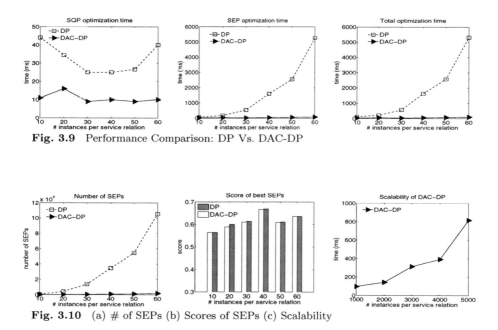

Fig. 3.9 Performance Comparison: DP Vs. DAC-DP

Fig. 3.10 (a) # of SEPs (b) Scores of SEPs (c) Scalability

Performance measure: We measure the performance of the optimization approaches using *computational time* and *score function value*. We use the formulae defined in Section 3.6.2 to compute the score of SEPs. We compare the scores of the best SEPs generated by the two query optimization

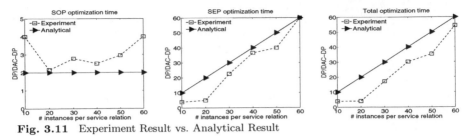

Fig. 3.11   Experiment Result vs. Analytical Result

algorithm. Since both query optimization algorithms both have two phases, we study and compare the computational time for each phase and the entire algorithm. We also investigate and compare the number of SEPs generated by each algorithm.

Figure 3.9 shows the optimization time resulting from the experiments. DP-DAC is much more efficient than DP due to the divide-and-conquer strategy. The chart on the left compares the optimization time for the first phase, where the most efficient service query plans (SQPs) are selected. The chart in the middle compares the optimization time for the second phase, where the best service execution plans (SEPs) are generated. DP-DAC outperforms DP in both cases. The right-hand-side chart compares the total optimization time.

Figure 3.10 (a) shows the number of SEPs generated by performing the most efficient SQP selected in the first phase. DP-DAC generates much less SEPs than DP. This also justifies why DP-DAC is more efficient in its second phase than DP. Figure 3.10 (b) shows the scores of the best SEPs generated by DP and DAC-DP. In two cases (number of instances 10 and 60), DP and DAC-DP output the best SEPs with the same score. In the other four cases, the scores of DAC-DP are slightly lower (less than three percent) than those of DP. The difference comes from the two approximation functions used by DAC-DP to aggregate QoWS parameters. We have conducted a set of additional experiments to further evaluate the scalability of the DAC-DP algorithm. We increase the number of instance per service relation with two orders of magnitude and test of the performance of DAC-DP with the number of service instances varying from 1000 to 5000. Experiment results (presented in Figure 3.10 (c)) show that DAC-DP can still perform very efficiently (using less than 1 second to query three service relations, each of which has 5000 service instances) on large number of service instances.

Compare with the analytical model: We further compare the experiment results with the results from the analytical model presented in Section 3.7. Although the analytical model only predicts the upper bound of the time complexity, we can still perform an approximate comparison. This is to justify that the experiment results follow the same trends as predicted by the analytical model. We focus on the improvement (in terms of optimization time) achieved by DAC-DP over DP. We define a variable DP/DAC-DP (i.e., the time used by DP divided by the time used by DAC-DP) to demonstrate the improvement. Figure 3.11 illustrates the detailed comparison results.

The chart on the left-hand-side shows the improvement for the first optimization phase. The complexity of this phase is mainly decided by the number of service relations under join. In our experiment settings, the DP approach needs to join three service relations whereas the DAC-DP only needs to join two service relations (the divide-and-conquer strategy removes the service relation *FI* from the join list by considering it separately). Therefore, in the analytical model, DP/DAC-DP should take an approximate value of $(2 \times N_{IO}^{DP})/N_{IO}^{DAC-DP}$, where N_{IO}^{DP} and N_{IO}^{DAC-DP} represent the number of interesting orders considered by DP and DAC-DP in the first optimization phase. Since the number of interested orders are unknown, they are not reflected by the analytical result in the chart (that is why the analytical result curve is a horizontal straight line). The actual experiment result curve stays above the analytical one. This is because DP joins one more service relations than DAC-DP, it naturally needs to consider more interesting orders, i.e., $N_{IO}^{DP}/N_{IO}^{DAC-DP} > 1$. This makes $(2 \times N_{IO}^{DP})/N_{IO}^{DAC-DP} > 2$.

The middle chart in Figure 3.11 shows the improvement in the second optimization phase. To calculate DP/DAC-DP for the analytical model, we use formulae (2) and (5) defined in Section 3.7. If we neglect the last item in formula (5) (i.e., $\sum_{i=N_{SR}^J+1}^{N_{SR}} N_{SI}^i$), we can derive that DP/DAC-DP takes an approximate value of N_{SR}^3, i.e., the number of service instances in the third service relation *FI*. Therefore, the analytical curve is an 45-degree straight line. The experiment curve has a very similar trends. It stays below the analytical curve because we neglect the last item in the denominator for the analytical curve. Since the total optimization time is dominated by the second phase, the total optimization time has a very similar trends as the second phase. The right-hand-side chart shows the result of the total optimization time.

Chapter 4
Multi-objective Service Query Optimization

Existing service optimization approaches usually select services based on a predefined objective function [59, 94]. They require users to express their preference over different (and sometimes conflicting) quality parameters as numeric *weights*. The objective function assigns a scalar value to each service provider based on the quality values and the weights given by the service user. The provider gaining the highest value from the objective function will be selected and returned to the user. Implementing such an optimization strategy may pose several challenges:

- Transforming personal preferences to numeric weights is a rather demanding task for users. Sometimes it is even impossible if the preference is still vague before the user is presented with the actual service providers. Users may miss their desired providers because of an imprecise specification of the weights, which would be very common in real-world scenarios.
- Users may lose the flexibility to select their desired providers by themselves. For example, a service user may choose a service provider that has a good reputation within a price range she can tolerate although price is a very important factor she considers. In this case, the relationship between reputation and price is subtle and the choice from different users may vary significantly. Therefore, it would be wise to give users the flexibility make their own selections from a small set of candidate providers.

Presenting users with all SEPs that meet the requirements in the service query may make users overloaded with too much information. Manually selecting the most suitable SEP from a large SEP space requires a painstaking and time-consuming process, which is also error prone. A promising direction is to present users with only *interesting* SEPs that both shrink the SEP space and guarantee that the user desired SEP will be included. A possible solution to tackle this problem is to use top-k queries. Instead of returning a single SEP, the top-k queries retrieve the best k SEPs. This greatly reduces the decision space and also gives users certain flexibility to make their own choice among the k SEPs. Top-k queries have been intensively investigated

Q. Yu and A. Bouguettaya, *Foundations for Efficient Web Service Selection*,
DOI 10.1007/978-1-4419-0314-3_4, © Springer Science+Business Media, LLC 2009

in the database community. Typical techniques include PREFER [42] and Onion [23] that rely respectively on pre-materialization and convex hulls. However, top-k queries are usually based on some specific preference function. Using top-k queries is not able to free users from assigning weight to different QoWS parameters. Therefore, they cannot completely address the above two issues.

We propose to use multi-objective service query optimization to deal with the above issues. We adopt a skyline computation approach to achieve multi-objective optimization. The remainder of this chapter is organized as follows. In Section 4.1, we present the concept of service skylines. In Section 4.2, we give an overview of the existing database skyline algorithms. In Section 4.3, we discuss the challenges for computing service skylines. We present the service skyline algorithms in Section 4.4. We experimentally evaluate and compare the proposed algorithms under different settings in Section 4.5.

4.1 The Service Skyline

A key observation is that the weighting mechanism is used for calculating a single objective function. Thus, we can free users from the weight assignment task if we do not use a single objective function to combine multiple QoWS parameters. In this case, we need to consider each user interested QoWS parameter individually and select the SEPs that are good at all these quality aspects. This turns out to be a multi-objective optimization problem. A natural solution is to incorporate the skyline operator in the proposed service query algebra. The skyline operator is coined in the database community [14]. Simply put, skyline consists of a set of objects that are not *dominated* by other objects. Object a dominates object b if a is better than b in at least one dimension and as good as or better than b in all other dimensions.

We use an example to illustrate how skyline can help resolve the issues of service query optimization. Suppose that Mary is interested in the economic and efficient SEPs., i.e., she wants the SEPs with minimum price and latency. All the points in Figure 4.1 represent the entire SEP space. The highlighted points, $\{a, b, c, d, e, f\}$, form the skyline of SEPs, which is also referred to as the *service skyline*. With the minimum condition, we can see that these SEPs are not dominated by any other SEP in the entire space. Therefore, they are preferable to other SEPs according to any scoring function that is monotone on all dimensions. For example, the skyline SEP d is better than the non-skyline SEP n because it is more efficient and cheaper. It is worth to note that this comparison is totally independent of the relative importance (i.e., weights) of the price and latency QoWS parameters. We further summarize the benefit offered by the skyline operator as follows:

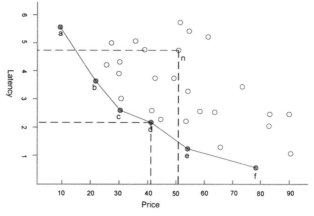

Fig. 4.1 Skyline of SEPs

- It completely frees users from the weight assignment task since the selection of SEPs is totally independent of the relative importance of different QoWS parameters.
- The skyline constitutes the SEP set that a service user is most interested in since all the non-skyline SEPs are dominated by the skyline ones.
- It gives users the flexibility to select their desired SEP from a relatively small decision space because the non-skyline SEPs (that usually constitute a large portion of the SEP space) will be eliminated by the skyline operator.

4.2 Computing Database Skylines: An overview

Before investigating how to find SEP skylines, we first give an overview of several existing approaches for computing database skylines. Typical algorithms include Block Nested Loops [14], Divide-and-Conquer [14], Bitmap [80], Index [80], and Nearest Neighbor [47, 60].

4.2.1 Block Nested Loops Algorithms

The block nested loops algorithm adopts a straightforward approach to tackle the skyline computation. It assumes no index structures (e.g., B-tree, R-tree, etc) of the data records. The skyline is computed iteratively through the direct comparison between data records. The algorithm keeps a set of candidate (i.e., incomparable) data records, called window, in the main memory. It then continuously loads the subsequent data record, say p, and compare it with the candidate records. There are three comparison results:

- If p is dominated by any record in the candidate window, it will be discarded immediately with no need to compare with any other candidate records or considered in future iterations.
- If some candidate records are dominated by p, all these records will be removed from the window and p will be inserted into the window.
- If p is incomparable with any record in the window, it will be inserted into the window.

As more data records are inserted into the candidate window, the size of the window may become larger than the main memory. In this case, the algorithm stores the extra incompatible data records into a temporary file. At the end of an iteration, all the data record inserted into the window before the creation of the temporary file are output as part of the skyline. The remaining data records in the window and the temporary file will go into the next iteration. This process continues until there are no remaining data records.

4.2.2 Divide-and-Conquer Algorithm

The divide-and-conquer algorithm takes full consideration of the limited capacity of the memory. The rationale is similar to the sort-merge algorithm that is used to sort large data files. The algorithm takes three major steps: split, compute, and merge.

- *Split* the entire dataset into k subsets, $P_1, ..., P_k$, along some dimension d so that each subset can fit into the memory.
- *Compute* the skyline of each subset using any main-memory algorithm and result in k sub-skylines $S_1, ..., S_k$.
- *Merge* the k sub-skylines into the final skyline.

Since the merged result may become larger than the memory, the split-compute-merge process may be applied in the merge step recursively. Each time this procedure is invoked, a different dimension will be selected to split the input dataset. The algorithm also avoids some unnecessary merges of sub-skylines because they are inherently incomparable due to the subset they reside in.

4.2.3 Bitmap Algorithm

The bitmap algorithm is proposed for progressively constructing the skylines. It uses a bitmap data structure to store all the necessary information to determine whether a record belongs to the skyline or not. The algorithm involves three major tasks: create bit vectors, transform bit vectors into bit-slices, and compute skylines. Bit-slices need only to be created once and then they can be used to calculate skylines for various queries.

- *Create bit vectors:* A d dimensional data record $x = (x_1, ..., x_d)$ is transformed as a m-bit vector. m equals the total number of distinct values over all the d dimensions, i.e., $m = \sum_{i=1}^{d} k_i$, where k_i is the number of distinct values in the ith dimension. Therefore, we have $x = (k_1 \text{ bits}, ..., k_d \text{ bits})$. Now, we investigate how to represent x_i with the k_i bits. Assume x_i is the j_ith distinct value on the ith dimension. Then in the k_i bits for x_i, the most significant $j_i - 1$ bits (i.e., bit 1 to $j_i - 1$) are set to 0 and the remaining bits are set to 1.
- *Transform bit vectors into bit-slices:* Instead of storing these bit vectors individually, the algorithm transposes all the transformed bit vectors into an array of so called *bit-slices*. The size of the array is m.
- *Compute skylines:* The algorithm uses bit-slices for efficient skyline computation. Consider a data record $x = (x_1, ..., x_d)$, where x_i is the j_ith distinct value on the ith dimension. The algorithm computes $C = BS_{1j_1} \& ... \& BS_{dj_d}$, where $\&$ is the bitwise "and" operation. BS_{ij_i} represents the bit-slice for the j_ith distinct value of the ith dimension. BS_{ij_i} has n bits, where n is the total number of data records. The kth bit of BS_{ij_i} is 1 if the kth data record ranks higher than or equal to j_i (which is the rank of x) on the ith dimension and it is 0 if otherwise. After the computation, the algorithm enumerates the number of '1's in C. If there is more than one '1' (which means except for itself, there are still other data records that are better than x in all the d dimensions, i.e., x is dominated by others), x is not in the skyline.

4.2.4 Index-based Algorithm

The index structures (e.g., B-tree, hash table, etc) on the data records can be used to facilitate the skyline computation. The first index-based algorithm is presented in [14]. The algorithm is based on B-tree and can be applied if there is an index for each dimension of the data records. Specifically, the computation proceeds as follows:

- *Locate the first skyline record:* The algorithm scan all the indexes in parallel until it locates the first data record that appears in all the dimensions.

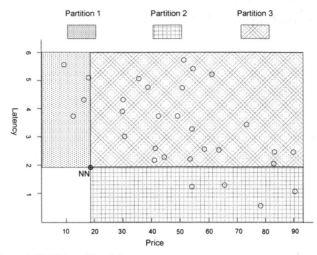

Fig. 4.2 Nearest Neighbor Algorithm

Since this data record is definitely in the skyline, it is immediately returned by the algorithm.

- *Remove the non-skyline records:* Take the index of the first dimension and scan the rest of the index entries after the entry of the returned data record. For a data record, if its index entries on all dimensions appear after the corresponding entries of the returned data record, this data record is not part of the skyline and should be removed.
- *Compute skyline for all other records:* For all other data records that have some index entries above the returned data records and the others below it, an existing skyline computation algorithm is applied to output other skyline records from them.

An improved version is presented in [80] that is able to progressively and more efficiently output the skyline. The key idea of this algorithm is to map a multi-dimensional data record into a single-dimensional data record. Consider a data record $x = (x_1, ..., x_d)$ and x_i has the minimum value among all dimensions. Then x will take value x_i and be assigned to a list, say l_i. There would be d such lists. Each list corresponds to one dimension because a value from any dimension could take a minimum value over the other dimensions for a data record. For each list, the algorithm sorts the data records in ascending order of the value in the corresponding dimension. Such an arrangement helps put the interesting data records near the top position of each list. A fast initial response time can thus be achieved. In addition, it also facilitates the elimination of a large body of non-skyline records. Specifically, if the maximum value across all dimensions of a data record is even smaller than the minimum value across all dimension of another data records, the latter should be eliminated.

Table 4.1 Major Database Skyline Algorithms

Index	Algorithm	Key Strategy
1	Block Nested Loop	Sequential scan
2	Divide-and-Conquer	Sort and partition
3	Bitmap	Bitmap structure
4	Index	B-tree based index
5	Nearest Neighbor	R-tree based index

4.2.5 Nearest Neighbor Algorithm

The nearest neighbor algorithm adopts a divide-and-conquer strategy to tackle the skyline computation. The key idea is to recursively apply nearest neighbor search to find the data record with the minimum distance from an imagined optimal data record (which is usually the beginning of the axes, i.e., the original point). Consider a set of two dimensional data records. The algorithm maintains a *to-do* list that stores the candidate data records. Initially, the to-do list contains the entire data space. The algorithm recursively uses the nearest neighbor search to compute the skyline and updates the to-do list. It terminates until the to-do list is empty. We elaborate on this process with the help of Figure 4.2.

1. Compute the near neighbor of data record $(0,0)$. The output data record is definitely part of the skyline and can be immediately returned to the user.
2. Divide the data space into different partitions. The region between NN and $(0,0)$ should be empty because otherwise NN will not be output as the nearest neighbor to $(0,0)$. There are three partitions that need to be considered. As we can see from Figure 4.2, all the data records fallen into partition 3 are all dominated by NN. Therefore, the entire partition 3 can be pruned away. Partition 1 and partition 2 will be regarded as two new sub data spaces and inserted into the to-do list.
3. For each partition in the to-do list, recursively apply Step 1 and 2, until the to-do list is empty.

The center of the nearest neighbor algorithm is to find the data record that has the minimum distance from an imagined optimal data record within a region (such as partition 1 and 2). The algorithm needs to rely on the R-tree based index structures [70, 8] for efficient computation of the nearest neighbor data record for a given region.

4.3 Challenges of Computing the SEP Skyline

A close investigation of the above database skyline algorithms helps achieve some interesting observations. This also identifies the inherent difference between database skylines and SEP skyline and highlights the challenges for computing the skyline of SEPs.

We summarize in Table 4.1 the underlying strategies adopted by each of the above algorithms for computing the database skylines. Each algorithm may have its own advantages and disadvantages. For example, algorithm 1 is usually most inefficient. However, it has the most widely applicability. Some of the algorithms also share key similarities. As we can see from Table 4.1, algorithms 2, 4, and 5 are able to leverage the index structure of the original data space to achieve more efficient computation of skylines. Among them, the index-based algorithms directly use B-tree (or B+-tree) to compute the skylines. The nearest neighbor algorithms use R-tree based index to efficiently perform the nearest neighbor search that indirectly accelerates the skyline computation process. For the divide-and-conquer algorithm, since it relies on sorting to partition the data space, an index structure can greatly improve its performance. Algorithm 3 relies on the bitmap structure to efficiently and progressively compute the skyline. Although bitmap is different from indexes (such as B-tree and R-tree), both of them are essentially data structures pre-computed from the original dataset. They just need to be constructed once (updates are sometimes required) and then can be applied to help efficiently resolve various types of skyline queries. Therefore, an interesting observation is that except for the Block Nested Loop algorithm, all the other skyline algorithms rely on some pre-computed data structures (i.e., bitmap, B-tree, R-tree) to achieve their efficiency of skyline computation.

The pre-computed data structures are tightly bounded with the original dataset. They capture the underlying characteristics of the original dataset in certain aspects that can be leveraged for efficiently compute the skylines. Although building these data structures are usually computationally expensive, the relative *static* property of the dataset enables the *one-time construction*, i.e., once the data structures are generated, they can be applied to almost all types of skyline queries. However, the *static* property does not hold for the SEP space any more. This poses a set of new challenges for computing SEP skylines:

1. In contrast to having single static SEP space, a new set of SEPs (i.e., a new SEP space) will be dynamically generated for any service query.
2. A SEP usually contains a set of member service operations. Different member service operations are selected for different service queries. More importantly, some member service operations may even not appear in the service queries. They are selected and put in the SEP based on the dependency constraints. Since service query optimization is based on user's preference on the entire SEP, the optimization of SEPs cannot be per-

formed based on the information carried by the service queries. Instead, the optimization needs to be carried out only after the SEPs have been generated.

3. The attributes of a SEP are aggregates of the corresponding attributes from its member service operations. Indices on the attributes of service relations (i.e., service operations) are usually not able to directly be applied to the aggregate attributes in the SEPs. Answering aggregate queries remains to be a challenging task in traditional database systems. It is usually addressed by leveraging materialized views [28, 39, 75]. However, view materialization may not be suitable for the highly dynamic service query optimization.

Example 4.1. Consider a service query that helps a user get a free insurance quote and a vehicle history report for less than 20 dollars. The service query needs to access both CP and CI and combine them to generate the final SEPs. We can use an algebraic expression to specify the query as follows:

$$\chi_{\{op_1, op_2\}}(\delta_{\lambda_4(op_1) \leq 20}(CP) \otimes \delta_{\lambda_4(op_2)=0}(CI))$$

where op_1 and op_2 represent the service operations historyReport *and* insuranceQuote *respectively. The service relation retrieved by the service query may consist of multiple service instances. Therefore, a corresponding number of SEPs will also be generated. Suppose there are K_1 CP service providers offering vehicle report for less than 20 dollars and K_2 CI service providers offering insurance quote for free. Thus, a total number of $K_1 \times K_2$ SEPs will be generated.* ∎

Example 4.1 highlights several important facts about service query optimization that helps understand the above research issues:

1. A SEP space (e.g., $K_1 \times K_2$ SEPs in Example 4.1) will be dynamically generated for each service query. Different service queries will have different SEP spaces.

2. A SEP may contain service operations that are not covered by the service query. For example, the service query only specifies historyReport and insuranceQuote since the service user is only interested in getting these functionalities. The query processor will automatically include drivingHistory and carQuote into the SEP based on the dependency constraints between these service operations. The service query optimization should consider all of the four service operations instead of only considering historyReport and insuranceQuote specified by the service query.

3. The quality attributes (e.g., latency, fee, etc) of a SEP are in fact the aggregate of the corresponding attributes of its member service operations. Table 3.4 gives the aggregation functions for calculating the quality of a SEP from the quality of service operations. For instance, in Example 4.1, the fee of a SEP is the sum of the fees of all the four service operations.

4.4 SEP Skyline Computation

We present a set of algorithms for computing SEP skylines in this section. Our first attempt is to extend the existing database skyline algorithms. These algorithms are based on the index structures (B+-tree, R-tree, etc) built upon the service relations. We identify the problems with these algorithms and propose a new indexing mechanism for service relations. We then continue to present a SEP skyline algorithm based on this new indexing structure.

Example 4.2. Consider a service query that helps users get insurance quote from car insurance services. The service query is specified as:

$$Q = \{s.sid, s[G(insuranceQuote)] | CI(s)\}$$

The resultant SEP in fact contains two service operations: drivingHistory, insuranceQuote *(denoted by op_1 and op_2 respectively).* drivingHistory *is included due to the dependency constraints. The service user wants a SEP with the lowest fee and quickest response time (i.e., min(fee) and min(latency)).*   ∎

We define a set of notations that will be used for explaining the algorithms:

- Aggregation (+): We use + to uniformly represent the aggregation of service operations. For example, the aggregation of two service operations op_1 and op_2 is denoted by $op_1 + op_2$.
- Domination (▷): The domination relationship between SEPs are denoted by ▷, i.e., $sep_1 ▷ sep_2$ means that sep_1 dominates sep_2. Suppose sep_1 has two service operations: op_1 and op_2. $sep_1 ▷^{op_1} sep_2$ means that sep_1 dominates sep_2 on op_1. Therefore, $sep_1 ▷ sep_2$ can also be represented as $sep_1 ▷^{op_1+op_2} sep_2$, i.e., sep_1 dominates sep_2 on the aggregation of op_1 and op_2. The negated notion, $sep_1 \not\triangleright sep_2$, means that sep_1 does not dominate sep_2. Similarly, $sep_1 \not\triangleright^{op_1} sep_2$ means that sep_1 does not dominate sep_2 on op_1.

Theorem 4.3. *For any two seps, sep_1 and sep_2, that contain k service operations $op_1,...,op_k$,*

$$(sep_1 ▷^{op_1} sep_2) \wedge ... \wedge (sep_1 ▷^{op_k} sep_2) \Rightarrow sep_1 ▷ sep_2$$

∎

An intuitive interpretation of Theorem 4.3 is that if all the service operations of sep_1 are better than those from sep_2, sep_1 dominates sep_2. However, the domination of sep_1 over sep_2 does not necessarily mean that all operations from sep_1 are better than those of sep_2, i.e., $sep_1 ▷ sep_2 \not\Rightarrow (sep_1 ▷^{op_1} sep_2) \wedge ... \wedge (sep_1 ▷^{op_k} sep_2)$. Instead, it only guarantees that the aggregation of operations in sep_1 is better than the aggregation of those from sep_2. Theorem 4.3 enables us to eliminate dominated SEPs from the SEP space. The basic strategy is to examine all the service operations in the SEPs and the SEPs with all operations dominated by others will be removed.

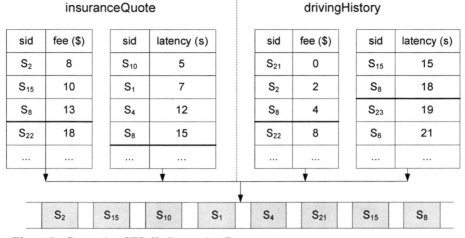

Fig. 4.3 Computing SEP Skylines using B-tree

4.4.1 Using B-trees

The most straightforward approach for computing SEP skylines is to extend the B-tree based approach [14]. A final SEP contains two service operations (`drivingHistory`, `insuranceQuote`) instead of only `insuranceQuote` specified by the service query. The user's requirement (i.e., lowest fee and quickest response time) is applied on the entire SEPs by considering the two operations simultaneously. To achieve this, we can take the fee and latency from the two member services as four different attributes, i.e., `drivingHistory.fee`, `drivingHistory.latency`, `insuranceQuote.fee`, and `insuranceQuote.latency`. We assume that these four attributes are all indexed using B-tree for efficient access. We can then scan the four indices simultaneously to find the first match of sid. All the service instances that are not inspected before the first match will be removed from further computation. The remained service instances will go through a second round selection to determine the final skyline. The second round selection needs to be conducted in a brute-force manner. The quality of a SEP (i.e., fee and latency, etc) will be calculated using the aggregate functions defined in Table 3.4. Then a non-index based approach (e.g., block nested loop, divide-and-conquer, etc) can be applied to compute the final skyline.

Figure 4.3 illustrates how to use the B-tree approach to compute the skyline of the example service query. The simultaneous scan identifies the first match, which is S_8. The uninspected *seps* are then eliminated. The scan process guarantees that, for any uninspected sep_k, $(sep_8 \triangleright^{op_1} sep_k) \wedge (sep_8 \triangleright^{op_2} sep_k)$ is true, where op_1 and op_2 are `drivingHistory` and `insuranceQuote` respectively. According to Theorem 4.3, $sep_8 \triangleright sep_k$ is true, i.e., sep_8 dominates sep_k. Therefore, sep_k should be removed from further computation.

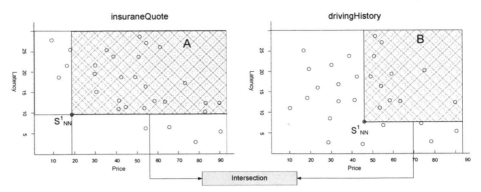

Fig. 4.4 Computing SEP Skylines using Nearest Neighbor Search

The remaining *seps* (i.e., S_2, S_{15},...,S_8) will go through the second round selection to generate the target skyline.

4.4.2 Nearest Neighbor Algorithm

We can also extend the nearest neighbor algorithm to compute skyline for service queries. We continue to use the sample service query to illustrate the computation process (see Figure 4.4).

1. Take the first member operation (i.e., `drivingHistory`) and compute the nearest neighbor of data record (0,0). Assume that the nearest neighbor we get is S_{NN}^1 and the set of *seps* dominated by S_{NN}^1 is A. We then take S_{NN}^1 and evaluate it on the second operation (i.e., `insuranceQuote`) and get the set of *seps* dominated by S_{NN}^1, which is B.
2. Compute the intersection of A and B and we get $C = A \cap B$. According to Theorem 4.3, all the *seps* in C are dominated by S_{NN}^1 and therefore should be removed from further computation.
3. For partition 1 and 2 (see Figure 4.2), recursively apply Step 1 and 2 to further remove dominated *seps*.
4. For the remaining *seps*, reverse the order of member operations (i.e., find the nearest neighbor of `insuranceQuote` and evaluate it on `drivingHistory`), and apply the above three steps.
5. Use a brute-force approach (similar to the one described in the B-tree approach) to generate the skyline from the remaining *seps*.

The above algorithm requires a frequent computation of intersections between two sets. Computing set intersections could be very expensive especially for large sets. Assume that the cardinalities of set A and B are k_1 and k_2 respectively. To get the intersection C, we usually need to do a pairwise comparison between these two sets that requires $O(k_1 \times k_2)$ time complexity. When k_1 and k_2 are large, this will be prohibitive as a frequent

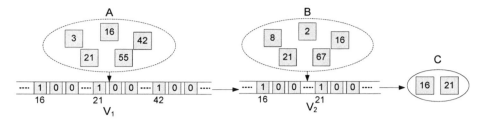

Fig. 4.5 Computing Set Intersections Using Bitmap

executed operation. Another approach is to sort the two sets and do a sequential pass simultaneously on them. This would require a time complexity of $O(k_1 \times log k_1 + k_2 \times log k_2)$.

We adopt the *key-indexed search* strategy to make this operation run in linear time. To achieve this efficiency, we need $O(n)$ additional space as a tradeoff. Suppose there are n service instances with the car insurance service. We assign the *id* numbers of these instances from 0 to n-1, i.e., $sid \in [0, n-1]$. The *id* numbers are distinct from each other. We use an assistance array T of size n to record these *sid*s. All the elements of the array are initialized to be 0. To compute the intersection of A and B, we first pass set A and add 1 the corresponding item of T accordingly. For example, if $sid_k \in A$, then set $T[sid_k]$ to 1 (the initial $T[sid_k]$ is 0). We then continue to apply the same process using B. In the end, all the *sid*s that satisfy $T[sid] > 1$ fall into the intersection. Obviously, the time complexity of this approach is $O(n)$.

We can further reduce the space complexity by using bitmaps to implement the assistance array T. Specifically, we can use two n-bits vectors V_1 and V_2 to replace T. They will only use $1/16$ of the space used by T. All the bits in V_1 and V_2 are initialized to 0. Similarly, we first pass A and set the corresponding bits of V_1 to 1 accordingly, i.e., if $sid_k \in A$, then $V_1[sid_k] = 1$. When we pass B, we set the bits in V_2 according to V_1, i.e., if $(sid_k \in B) \land (V_1[sid_k] == 1)$, then $V_2[sid_k] = 1$. Finally, all the *sid*s that satisfy $V_2[sid] == 1$ fall into the intersection. We can use bitwise operators to implement the bit vectors. This enables to process bits in a batch mode that can also make it run more efficiently.

Analysis

Theorem 4.3 offers us heuristics for pruning dominated *seps*. However, algorithms based on Theorem 4.3 may be far less efficient than an optimal algorithm. They have to use a brute-force approach on a usually large *sep* space due to the limited prune power of the adopted heuristics. In this section, we conduct an analysis that gives an insight of this inherent inefficiency.

We continue to use Example 4.2. For two *seps*, if sep_1 dominates sep_2, it can be represented as $sep_1 \triangleright sep_2$. Since there are two membership operations in the *seps*, $sep_1 \triangleright sep_2$ actually means $sep_1 \triangleright^{op_1+op_2} sep_2$. There are four possible situations that lead to $sep_1 \triangleright^{op_1+op_2} sep_2$:

1. $(sep_1 \triangleright^{op_1} sep_2) \wedge (sep_1 \triangleright^{op_2} sep_2)$
2. $(sep_1 \triangleright^{op_1} sep_2) \wedge (sep_1 \ntriangleright^{op_2} sep_2)$
3. $(sep_1 \ntriangleright^{op_1} sep_2) \wedge (sep_1 \triangleright^{op_2} sep_2)$
4. $(sep_1 \ntriangleright^{op_1} sep_2) \wedge (sep_1 \ntriangleright^{op_2} sep_2)$

Theorem 4.3 only covers the first situation, i.e., $(sep_1 \triangleright^{op_1} sep_2) \wedge (sep_1 \triangleright^{op_2} sep_2) \Rightarrow sep_1 \triangleright^{op_1+op_2} sep_2$. We can directly eliminate sep_2 if the first situation is satisfied. However, for the remaining three situations, we have to postpone the decision until the aggregate attributes of the *seps* are actually computed and compared. Therefore, the heuristics derived from Theorem 4.3 only helps prune a (sometimes small) subset of *seps*. For a correlated service base, where some service instances that are good in one dimension are also good in the other dimensions, the heuristics may have a good prune capability because there may be few very good service instances that dominate others. However, for other service bases, (e.g., independent or anti-correlated) the prune power may be very limited.

Among all the above database skyline algorithms, the nearest neighbor algorithm outperforms others in terms of overall performance and general applicability independently of the dataset characteristics. The nearest neighbor search depends on a R-tree to gain its efficiency. BBS (branch and bound skyline) [60], which is another R-tree based approach, further improves the nearest neighbor algorithm. It is an optimal algorithm in terms of node accesses. Since the R-tree based algorithms are among the best skyline computation approaches, we take interest in extending these algorithms or building algorithms based on R-trees to efficiently compute the service skyline.

4.4.3 Extending BBS

BBS (branch and bound skyline) is a database skyline algorithm that leverages a priority queue (or a heap) and an in-memory R-tree to efficiently and progressively retrieve the skyline [60]. The heap helps determine the order of retrieving the data points whereas the in-memory R-tree is for dominance checking (i.e., removing the dominated data points).

We propose in this section an algorithm (called BBS4SEP) that extends BBS. By making several key changes on BBS, BBS4SEP is able to efficiently retrieve SEP skylines. Suppose that a service space is indexed by a R-tree. In Example 4.2, the SEPs can be regarded as having four dimensions (i.e., op_1.fee, op_1.latency, op_2.fee, and op_2.latency) and organized in a R-tree. The leaf nodes of the R-tree represents the SEPs. An intermediate node represents a minimum bounding rectangle (MBR) of each node at its lower level. The heap is constructed to efficiently output the node (intermediate or leaf node) that has the least *mindist*. The *mindist* of a leaf node is the summation of all its coordinate values whereas the *mindist* of an intermediate node is the *mindist* of its lower-left corner point.

BBS4SEP works as follows (shown in Algorithm 7). It initially inserts all the entries in the root of the R-tree into the heap H. It then iteratively expands these entries based on their *mindist*. The expanded entry will be removed from the heap whereas its child entries will be inserted. When the first leaf node is returned, it will be inserted into the resultant skyline list L. The in-memory R-tree IR will then be initialized using the first skyline point. It worth to note that BBS4SEP has a similar behavior as BBS up to this step. The IR has a different structure as that of BBS. Recall that if SEP_1 dominates SEP_2, it actually means $SEP_1 \triangleright^{op_1 + op_2} SEP_2$. Since the IR is used for dominance checking, it should be able to prune SEPs based on the aggregate attributes of SEPs. Therefore, the IR will be dynamically constructed with two dimensions: SEP.fee and SEP.latency, where

$$SEP.fee = op_1.fee + op_2.fee \tag{4.1}$$

$$SEP.latency = op_1.latency + op_2.latency \tag{4.2}$$

After the IR is constructed, the entries output from the heap will be checked against the IR for dominance. Specifically, if a top entry in the heap is dominated by some SEP in the IR tree, it can be directly pruned. Otherwise, 1) it will be expanded into several child entries if it is an intermediate node and these child entries will also be checked for dominance against the IR before inserting into the heap because the dominated entries can also be directly pruned; 2) it will inserted into L and IR if it is a leaf node.

Algorithm 7 BBS4SEP

Require: A R-tree RT
Ensure: A list of the SEP skyline points L
 1: $L = \phi$, $IR = \phi$, $H = \phi$
 2: **while** $H \neq \phi$ **do**
 3:     $e = H.extractmin()$;
 4:     **if** $IR \neq \phi$ **then**
 5:         map e to the dimensions of IR and check dominance;
 6:         **if** e is dominated **then**
 7:             prune e;
 8:         **else**
 9:             **if** e is an intermediate node **then**
10:                 **for** each child entry $e.c_i$ of e **do**
11:                     **if** $e.c_i$ is not dominated by IR **then**
12:                         $H.insert(e.c_i)$;
13:                     **end if**
14:                 **end for**
15:             **else**
16:                 $L.insert(e)$;
17:                 $IR.insert(e)$;
18:             **end if**
19:         **end if**
20:     **else**
21:         **if** e is an intermediate node **then**
22:             **for** each child entry $e.c_i$ of e **do**
23:                 $H.insert(e.c_i)$;
24:             **end for**
25:         **else**
26:             $L.insert(e)$;
27:             initialize IR using e;
28:         **end if**
29:     **end if**
30: **end while**

Analysis

The IR tree enables dominance checking on the aggregate attributes of SEPs. It determines the SEP *skyline search region (SSR)* that is the section of the data space containing the skyline SEPs [60]. By observing formulae (1) and (2), we find that the R-tree (denoted by RT) that is used to index the service space and the in-memory R-tree IR share the same *mindist*, i.e.,

$$mindist = SEP.fee + SEP.latency =$$
$$op_1.fee + op_2.fee + op_1.latency + op_2.latency$$

Property 4.4. Given a R-tree (RT) that indexes the service space, BBS4SEP only accesses candidate entries in the R-tree that potentially contain skyline SEPs if RT and the in-memory R-tree (IR) share the same mindist function.

PROOF: *A candidate entry should intersect with the* SSR. *On the other hand, a non-candidate entry e does not overlap with the* SSR. *This implies that there is a skyline SEP ψ that can dominate the lower-left corner of e. ψ must also have a* mindist *that is smaller than that of e [60]. We use the notion* mindist(IR) *to denote the* mindist *calculated under the in-memory R-tree* IR. *Similarly, we use the notion* mindist(RT) *to denote the* mindist *calculated under* RT. *Recall that the heap enables that the entries in the* RT *are visited in ascending order of their* mindists. *If* mindist(IR) *equals to* mindist(RT), *it can be guaranteed that ψ is processed before e so that e is pruned by ψ. In this manner, the non-candidate entries will be pruned and only candidate ones are accessed.* ∎

Given Property 4.4, we can estimate the number of nodes accessed by BBS4SEP. Assume that the height of RT is h and there are $cand_i$ candidate nodes in the ith level of the R-tree. The total number of node accesses can be represented as

$$NA = \sum_{i=0}^{h-1} cand_i \tag{4.3}$$

To further examine how NA is related to the structure of the R-tree and the inherent characteristics of the data space, we further elaborate (6.17). Specifically, h can be specified as $1 + \lceil log_f(\frac{N}{f}) \rceil$, where N is the cardinality of the data space and f is the average fanout of a node in RT. Suppose there are n_i nodes at level i and the probability that a node at level i intersects with SSR is $P^i_{intsect(SSR)}$. The candidate nodes at level i can be described as [60]

$$cand_i = n_i \times P^i_{intsect(SSR)} \tag{4.4}$$

The number of node at level i can be specified as $n_i = \frac{N}{f^{i+1}}$. $P^i_{intsect(SSR)}$ can be evaluated by using the node density $D_i(p)$ at level i, i.e.,

$$P^i_{intsect(SSR)} = \int_{p \in SSR} D_i(p)dp \tag{4.5}$$

A pessimistic upper bound for retrieving the entire skyline is given by [60] , which is $|L| \times h$. It is decided by the cardinality of the skylines (i.e., $|L|$) and the height of RT. This upper bound corresponds to the situation that the algorithm needs to go through a complete path (i.e., the length of the path is h) to find each skyline point. However, multiple skyline points may be grouped into a single node or belong to the same branch of the R-tree. In this regard, the R-tree can be viewed as a *cluster* mechanism that groups together the points with similar properties (e.g., similar coordinate values). Since the total number of node accesses is less than $|L| \times h$, we can have

$$NA = \alpha \times |L| \times h = \sum_{i=0}^{\lceil log_f(\frac{N}{f}) \rceil} \frac{N}{f^{i+1}} \times \int_{p \in SSR} D_i(p)dp \tag{4.6}$$

where $\alpha \in (0, 1]$ is defined as a bounding factor. From (6.17), (6.18), and (6.19), we can see that NA is determined by the cardinality of the data space, the node density of each level of the R-tree, and the fanout of the R-tree. Therefore, α is related to the structure of the R-tree and the inherent characteristics of the data space.

The above analysis helps us further investigate the performance of BBS4SEP. Although it has an upper bound of $|L| \times h$, it may not be an optimal solution for retrieving the SEP skylines (i.e., the bounding factor α of BBS4SEP may be large). The reason is that BBS4SEP is based on a R-tree (i.e., RT) that is constructed from the original service space. The service space is different from the SEP space whose coordinates are the aggregates of the service space. Therefore, (1) the SEP space may have different characteristics with the original service space; (2) a R-tree built from the SEP space (where we try to find the skylines) may have a different structure with a R-tree built from the original service space. We illustrate these two aspects by using two simple examples.

4.4.3.1 Characteristics of the data space

Let's continue to use Example 4.2. Based on (2), the latency of a SEP is the sum of the latency from its member operations. We use X and Y to represent the latency of the two member operations and assume they are two independent continuous random variables with density functions $f_X(x)$ and $f_Y(y)$. The latency of the SEP is described as the sum of X and Y, i.e., $Z = X + Y$. The density function of Z is $f_Z(z)$ with $f_Z = f_X * f_Y$, where $*$ is the *convolution* operator. Specifically,

$$f_Z(z) = (f_X * f_Y)(z) = \int_{-\infty}^{+\infty} f_X(z - y) f_Y(y) dy$$

As an example to show how the distribution of Z is different from X and Y, we assume X and Y are randomly chosen variables from interval $[0,1]$ with uniform probability density. $Z = X + Y$ is the sum of these two variables. The density functions of X and Y are described as:

$$f_X(x) = f_Y(y) = \begin{cases} 1 \text{ if } 0 \leq x \leq 1 \\ 0 \text{ otherwise} \end{cases}$$

The density function of Z can be computed from the *convolution* of f_X and f_Y:

$$f_Z(z) = \int_{-\infty}^{+\infty} f_X(z - y) f_Y(y) dy = \begin{cases} z & \text{if } 0 \leq z \leq 1 \\ 2 - z & \text{if } 1 \leq z \leq 2 \\ 0 & \text{otherwise} \end{cases}$$

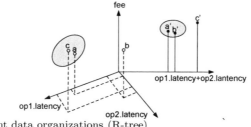

Fig. 4.6   Different data organizations (R-tree)

We can see that Z has a triangle distribution that is different from both f_X and f_Y. We use this example just to show that how the characteristics of the SEP space may be different from the original service space.

4.4.3.2 Structure of the R-tree

The R-trees may organize service instances in different ways in the SEP space as compared to the original service space. Using Example 4.2, we assume that all the service instances provide the insurance quote for free (i.e., op$_2$.fee=0). This enables us to visualize the SEPs in the original service space (with three dimensions because the op$_2$.fee dimension is collapsed into the origin). As we can see in Figure 4.6, the service space is represented using three coordinates: fee, op$_1$.latency, and op$_2$.latency. We select three representative SEPs, a, b, and c to investigate how they could be organized differently in the original service space and the SEP space. In the service space, a and b are far from each other because they have quite different values for the latency on their two member operations, i.e., a is much more efficient on performing op$_2$ whereas b is much more efficient on performing op$_1$. Another SEP c is much nearer to a than b although it is less efficient on performing both op$_1$ and op$_2$ than a. Therefore, a and c may be more likely to be "clustered" into the same MBR by a R-tree built from the original service space. However, in the SEP space (represented using two coordinates: fee and op$_1$.latency+op$_2$.latency in Figure 4.6), a is actually much closer to b than c. In this case, a and b may be more likely to be "clustered" into the same MBR by a R-tree built from the SEP space. If both a and b belong to the SEP skyline, they can be retrieved together. In contrast, retrieving a and b from the original service space may require more node accesses because they could be in different leaf nodes or even different branches of the R-tree.

4.4.3.3 Summary

BBS4SEP is based on an index structure (i.e., a R-tree) built from the original service space. The above analysis shows that: (1) the underlying character-istics (e.g., data distribution) of the service space and the SEP space are different; (2) a R-tree (say R_1) built from the service space may organize SEPs into different ways than a R-tree (say R_2) built from the SEP space. From (6.20) we observe that the number of node accesses is related to the cardinality of the data space, the fanout of the R-tree, and the node density of each level of the R-tree. Since the cardinality stays the same (i.e., the number of SEPs) and we can also make R_1 and R_2 have the same average fanout, the node density of each level of R_1 and R_2 will be different due to (1) and (2). This accounts for the performance difference (in terms of node access) of BBS4SEP.

4.4.4 Operation Graph based Indexing (OGI)

An effective improvement on BBS4SEP is to make it perform on a R-tree that is constructed directly from the SEP space. However, the challenge is that the SEP space is dynamically generated by each service query. This makes the SEP space inherently different from the original service space which is relatively static. Pre-computing an index structure for such a dynamic space seems to be infeasible.

In this section, we present an operation graph based indexing (OGI) approach to build indices for SEPs. Although different SEP spaces can be dynamically formed for different service queries, SEPs are not generated in an *ad hoc* manner. The dependency constraints between service operations only allow SEPs that conform to certain *patterns* to be generated. These patterns are like rules that define what kind of SEPs can be generated. If we know these patterns in advance, we can *foresee* the properties (i.e., the aggregate attributes) of the SEPs and construct index structures on them. Now the problem turns out to be whether such patterns exist or not and if yes, how to find such patterns. The proposed service model provides a natural solution for this problem.

Lemma 4.5. *Consider a set of SEPs, $SEP_1,...,SEP_k$, that are generated from service relation SR with k service instances. Assume that these SEPs are used to access operation op specified by some service query. The operation graph $G(op)$ and service relation SR carry enough information to construct the index for the SEPs.*

PROOF: Recall Theorem 3.10. The operation graph $G(op)$ consists of a minimum number of necessary operations that make *op* accessible. Thus, $G(op)$ identifies all the operations (i.e., *op* and all its dependent operations) in the SEPs. The service instances in SR store the QoWS parameters for each of these operations. Combining them, the aggregate QoWS parameters of SEPs can be computed using Table 3.4. Indices can thus be constructed from the QoWS parameters of SEPs.   ∎

Operation graph based indexing (OGI) enables us to pre-compute indices for SEPs. Algorithms built from OGI can thus use an index on the SEP space. This has two major advantages over BBS4SEP:

- OGI overcomes the "distortions" (e.g., the characteristics of data space and structure of the R-tree) introduced by using an index on the original service space.
- A R-tree index on the SEP space has lower dimensionality than a R-tree on the service space. The former has a dimensionality that equals to the number of user interested quality attributes while the dimensionality of the latter equals the number of user interested quality attributes times the service operations in a SEP.

4.5 Experimental Study

We conduct an extensive set of experiments to assess the effectiveness of the proposed service skyline computation algorithms. We run our experiments on a cluster of *Sun Enterprise Ultra 10* workstations with 512 Mbytes Ram under *Solaris* operating system. The node capacity of the R-trees is 100. The QoWS attributes[1] of service instances are generated in three different ways following the approach described in [14]: 1) *Independent QoWS* where all the QoWS attributes of service instances are uniformly distributed, 2) *Anti-correlated QoWS* where a service instance is good at one of the QoWS attributes but bad in one or all of the other QoWS attributes, and 3) *Correlated QoWS* where a service instance which is good at one of the QoWS attributes is also good at the other QoWS attributes.

We setup a set of experiment parameters to evaluate and compare the performance of BBS4SEP and OGI. These include the number of QoWS attributes in the range of 2 to 5, the number of operations per SEP in the range of 2 to 5, and the cardinality of the service relations in the range of 100k to 500k (i.e., 100,000 to 500,000). We also study the performance of skyline computation over multiple services and investigate how the performance varies with different number of services in a SEP. By performance, we report both the node accesses (which is independent of hardware settings) and the actual running time on our experiment machines. Finally, we study the sizes of the SEP skylines and examine whether they are in a practical range for user selection.

---

[1] We use QoWS attributes instead of QoWS parameters in the experiment section to differentiate it from the term "experiment parameters" we use in this section.

4.5.1 Number of QoWS Attributes

We study the effect of the number of QoWS attributes in this section. We keep the cardinality as 100k, the number of operation per SEP as 2, and vary the number of attributes from 2 to 5. Figure 4.7 and 4.8 show how the number of node accesses and the actual running time vary with the number of attributes for both independent and anti-correlated QoWS. OGI outperforms BBS4SEP on small number of attributes by almost an order of magnitude but the difference decreases as the number of attributes increases. The performance difference comes from two sources: 1) BBS4SEP works on a R-tree built from the original service space (as contrast to a R-tree built from the SEP space used by OGI); 2) The R-tree used by BBS4SEP has a dimensionality which is two times (since the number of operations per SEP is 2 in this case) of the one used by OGI. The difference becomes smaller with a larger number of attributes, which is due to that both algorithms are dominated by the poor performance of R-tree in high dimensions.

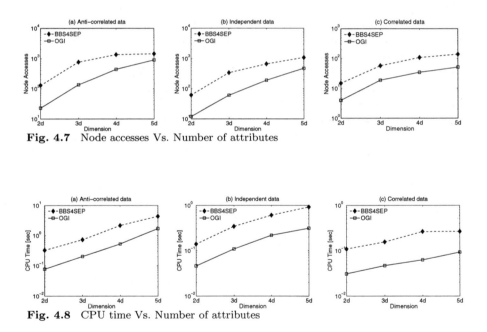

Fig. 4.7   Node accesses Vs. Number of attributes

Fig. 4.8   CPU time Vs. Number of attributes

4.5.2 Number of Operations per SEP

We study the effect of the number of operations per SEP with Figure 4.9 and 4.10. We keep the cardinality as 100k, the number of QoWS attributes as 2, and vary the number of operations per SEP from 2 to 5. OGI is more efficient than BBS4SEP with several orders of magnitude and the difference increases with the number of operations. The performance degradation of BBS4SEP is mainly due to the dimensionality increment of the R-tree with the number of operations. A close investigation reveals that the performance of OGI is insensitive to the number of operations. By using the operation graph to index the SEPs, the same QoWS attributes from multiple operations (e.g., the fee of operations) are aggregated into a single QoWS attribute of the SEP (e.g., the fee of a SEP). Therefore, the dimensionality of the R-tree used by OGI equals to a constant (i.e., the number of different QoWS attributes which is 2 in this case) and will not increase with the number of operations.

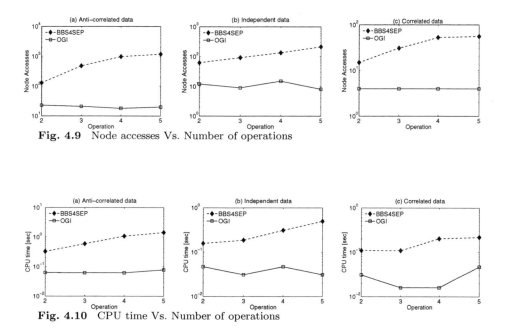

Fig. 4.9 Node accesses Vs. Number of operations

Fig. 4.10 CPU time Vs. Number of operations

4.5.3 Cardinality of Service Relations

We show the effect of cardinality in Figure 4.11 and 4.12. We keep the number of QoWS attributes as 2, the number of operations per SEP as 2, and vary the cardinality from 100k to 500k. OGI outperforms BBS4SEP by almost an order of magnitude due to similar reasons as described in Section 4.5.1. Both algorithms do not exhibit an obvious performance degradation with the increment of cardinality. For some cases, the algorithms even perform more

efficiently with larger cardinality which is due to the positions of the skyline
SEPs and the order they are retrieved [60].

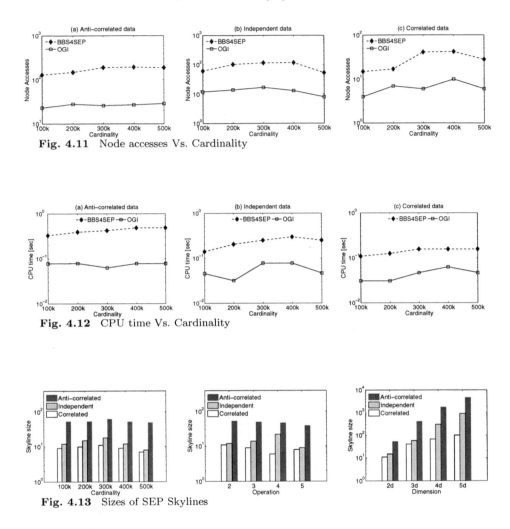

Fig. 4.11   Node accesses Vs. Cardinality

Fig. 4.12   CPU time Vs. Cardinality

Fig. 4.13   Sizes of SEP Skylines

4.5.4 Sizes of the SEP Skylines

We finally examine how the sizes of SEP skylines change with cardinality,
number of operations per SEP, number of QoWS attributes, and number
of services. Figure 4.13 presents some interesting effects of these parameters
on the sizes of SEP skylines. First of all, the skylines generated from anti-
correlated QoWS have larger sizes than those generated from independent

and correlated QoWS, which is just as expected. Second, cardinality and number of operations per SEP have no obvious effect on the sizes of SEP skylines. As the cardinality varies from 100k to 500k, the sizes of skylines for independent and correlated QoWS vary from 5 to 20 whereas those for anti-correlated QoWS vary from 30 to 40. The sizes of skylines stay in a similar range respectively when we vary the number of operations per SEP from 2 to 5. Interestingly, the sizes of skylines for anti-correlated QoWS have a trend to decrease with the number of operations. This may be due to that the aggregation of QoWS attributes from multiple operations compromises the anti-correlated effect. Third, the sizes of skylines clearly increase with the number of QoWS attributes and the number of services. However, in most practical usage scenarios where the number of QoWS attributes and the number of services are less than three, the sizes of the skylines are still within a practical range for user selection.

Chapter 5
Skyline Computation for Multi-Service Query Optimization

In this chapter, we study a more general and challenging problem: *computing service skylines over sets of services*. Following Example 1.2 described in Chapter 1, a complex service package (like a trip package) is formed by combining services from different providers (e.g., TripPlanner, Map, and Weather). The possible combinations of service providers will increase exponentially with the number of services involved. Suppose that there are $n_1,...,$ and n_m providers for each of the m services in a service package. To find the skyline for the service package, $\prod_{i=1}^{m} n_i$ number of candidates need to be evaluated. The computational cost would be prohibitive if the following conditions are true: (C_1) the number of services in a service package is large, i.e., m is large; (C_2) the number of providers for each service is large, i.e., n_i is large.

An intuitive solution that addresses the above challenge is to compute the multi-service skylines from single service skylines. This solution is valid due to two observations: (O_1) a multi-service skyline point can only be formed by a set of single service skyline points; (O_2) the sizes of skylines are usually much smaller than the sizes of the service space (i.e., the number of providers). In this case, only $\mathcal{N} = \prod_{i=1}^{m} k_i$ maximum number of candidates need to be evaluated due to O_1, where k_i is the size of the ith service skyline and we expect that $k_i \ll n_i$ due to O_2. Thus, the computational cost can be reduced with several orders of magnitude. However, $\mathcal{N}$ can still be large as more services are involved in the service package. In this chapter, we present a progressive and pipelineable approach for computing multi-service skylines, which also has a nearly optimal time complexity. The major contributions are summarized as follows:

- We first develop a baseline algorithm (referred to as *one pass algorithm* or OPA), which performs a single pass on the $\mathcal{N}$ candidates and outputs the skyline when the pass is complete. It employs a special enumeration mechanism to effectively reduce the number of false positive skyline points during skyline computation.
- We present a *dual progressive algorithm* (referred to as DPA) that is completely pipelineable and able to progressively report the skyline. It lever-

Q. Yu and A. Bouguettaya, *Foundations for Efficient Web Service Selection*, DOI 10.1007/978-1-4419-0314-3_5, © Springer Science+Business Media, LLC 2009

ages an expansion tree and a parent table to ensure the efficiency and progressiveness.

- We develop a *bottom-up approach* (referred to as BUA) that extends DPA through an early pruning strategy. BUA is able to compute the skyline with a nearly optimal time complexity. With early pruning, BUA also exhibits a good scalability with the increment of the number of services.
- We perform a rigorous analytical study and conduct an extensive set of experiments to evaluate the proposed multi-service skyline computation algorithms.

The remainder of this chapter is organized as follows. We formally define the multi-service skyline computation problem in Section 5.1. We present one pass algorithm, dual progressive algorithm, and the bottom-up approach in Sections 5.2, 5.3, and 5.4, respectively. We present the experimental results in Section 5.5.

5.1 Preliminaries

A complex service package (e.g., a travel package) typically requires access to a set of operations across multiple services. As stated in the beginning of this chapter, computing a SEP skyline for such a service package would incur intensive computational overhead. We present our approaches to efficiently compute service skylines over sets of services. For clarity, we use the term SEP to specifically refer to the service execution plan for a single service and the SEP skyline refers to the skyline for a single service. We use the term MEP to refer to the service execution plan for sets of services. Therefore, we study the problem of *efficiently computing the MEP skylines* in this section. Table 6.2 summarizes the terminologies used throughout the chapter.

Table 5.1 Terminologies

Term	Definition
SEP	service execution plan for a single service
MEP	service execution plan for sets of services
SK_i	the ith SEP skyline
k_i	size of the ith SEP skyline
score	the sum of the QoWS attributes of a MEP(SEP)
$\mathcal{MS}$	the MEP skyline
$A \rhd B$	A dominates B
$\mathcal{N}$	size of the MEP space
m	number of services
d	number of QoWS attributes

PROBLEM DEFINITION. Given m services with d user interested QoWS attributes, where the ith service has n_i different providers, the problem of *MEP skyline computation* is to compute the service skyline $\mathcal{MS}$ over the m services.

Computing the MEP skyline in a brute force manner is computationally intensive. The following observation helps improve the computation efficiency directly.

Lemma 5.1. *Given m services $S_1, ..., S_m$ and the set of SEP skylines $SK_1, ..., SK_m$, computed for each of them, the MEP skyline $\mathcal{MS}$ over $S_1, ..., S_m$ can be completely decided by $SK_1, ..., SK_m$.* ∎

Lemma 5.1 enables us to compute the MEP skylines by only considering the SEP skylines. We develop a one pass algorithm based on this. It performs a single pass on the MEP space with a size of $\mathcal{N} = \prod_{i=1}^{m} k_i$ to compute the MEP skyline.

5.2 One Pass Algorithm

We present a *One Pass Algorithm* (OPA) in this section. During the single pass of the MEP space, OPA enumerates the candidate MEPs one by one and only stores the potential skyline MEPs. It outputs the skyline after all the candidate MEPs have been evaluated. OPA requires that all the SEP skylines are sorted according to the scores of the SEPs. OPA works as follows (shown in Algorithm 8). It starts by evaluating the first MEP (referred to as MEP_1) that is formed by combining the top SEPs from each SEP skyline. It is guaranteed that $MEP_1 \in \mathcal{MS}$ because MEP_1 has the minimum score in the MEP space so that no other MEPs can dominate it. With the minimum score, MEP_1 is expected to have a very good pruning capacity. Thus, OPA puts MEP_1 on the top of $\mathcal{MS}$ so that the non-skyline MEPs which are dominated by MEP_1 can be pruned at the earliest time. After this, OPA continues to enumerate all other MEPs, one by each time. For each MEP_i, the algorithm checks it against the current $\mathcal{MS}$. When MEP_i meets the first MEP, say MEP_j, that can dominate it, the algorithm prunes MEP_i and stops further checking. On the other hand, if MEP_i dominates any MEP, say MEP_j, in $\mathcal{MS}$, MEP_j will be removed from the skyline. If none of the MEPs in $\mathcal{MS}$ can dominate MEP_i, MEP_i will be inserted into the skyline.

Algorithm 8 One Pass Algorithm

Require: m sorted SEP skylines $SK_1, ..., SK_m$
Ensure: The MEP skyline $\mathcal{MS}$

```
 1: N = 1; {number of candidate MEPs}
 2: for all i ∈ [2,N] do
 3:     MEP_i = EnumerateNext(SK_1,...,SK_m);
 4:     IsDominated = False;
 5:     for all j ∈ [1,|MS|] do
 6:         MEP_j = MS.get(j);
 7:         if MEP_i ▷ MEP_j then
 8:             MS.remove(j);
 9:         else if MEP_j ▷ MEP_i then
10:             IsDominated = True;
11:             break;
12:         end if
13:     end for
14:     if IsDominated == False then
15:         MS.add(MEP_i);
16:     end if
17: end for
```

One outstanding issue with OPA is the *false positive* skyline MEPs, which incur additional space and CPU cost. The false positives are generated because OPA has no restriction on the enumeration order of the MEPs. Some early discovered MEP that has been inserted into the skyline may be dominated by other later discovered MEPs. These false positive MEPs will stay in the skyline (which introduces space cost) and be compared with all the MEPs discovered after them until being dominated (which introduces CPU cost).

To reduce the number of false positives, we add some special control on the EnumerateNext function of DPA. Suppose that there are m SEP skylines (each of them are sorted on the scores of its SEPS). EnumerateNext first returns MEP_1. It then keeps increasing the index of the mth SEP skyline to enumerate the remaining MEPs. When the index hits the end of the mth SEP skyline, the index of $(m-1)$th SEP skyline will increase by 1 and the index of the mth skyline will reset to 0. This will propagate to all other SEP skylines until all MEPs are enumerated. Since all the SEP skylines are sorted, this process tends to enumerate the MEPs by roughly following the ascending order of their scores. The effectiveness of the EnumerateNext function is justified by our experimental results.

5.3 Dual Progressive Algorithm

We present a $\underline{D}$ual $\underline{P}$rogressive $\underline{A}$lgorithm (DPA) in this section. The underlying principle of DPA is the *dual progressive strategy*, which we briefly elaborate as follows.

- DPA *progressively* enumerates the MEPs in an ascending order of their *scores*. By "progressively", we mean that it does not need any presorting, which is usually very time consuming and thus blocks on input [26, 37]. DPA "intelligently" retrieves the MEPs based on their *scores* one at a time. This is non-trivial if the entire MEP space is not initially sorted. DPA follows the enumeration steps defined by an *expansion tree* and leverages a set of key data structures to achieve this, which will be explained in what follows.
- DPA *progressively* reports the skyline MEPs. By "progressively", we mean that once a MEP is discovered not being dominated by any existing skyline MEP, it is guaranteed to be in the skyline and can be returned to the user. This also implies that no false positives are generated by DPA. This is because that a later discovered MEP_j cannot have a smaller *score* than an earlier discovered MEP_i due to the first progressive property of DPA. Based on the definition of *score*, it is impossible for MEP_j to dominate MEP_i because otherwise the former should have a smaller *score* than the latter.

The dual progressive property helps DPA gain two major advantages: (1) DPA is a completely pipelineable algorithm, i.e., it does not block on both input and output. It does not block on input because presorting is no longer needed. Meanwhile, the progressive generation of the skyline make it non-block on output. (2) Since only true skyline MEPs are kept in $\mathcal{MS}$, the space overhead is greatly reduced. In addition, many useless comparisons are expected to be eliminated.

5.3.1 Basic Progressive Enumeration

The second progressive property is essentially a natural result from the first progressive property. We focus on investigating how the first progressive property is achieved in this section. Similar to OPA, DPA also requires that the SEP skylines are all sorted. The entire MEP space can be enumerated systematically using a MEP expansion tree. Figure 5.1 shows the expansion tree for three SEP skylines, $A(a_1, a_2, a_3)$, $B(b_1, b_2, b_3)$, and $C(c_1, c_2, c_3)$. The number of MEPs generated from these skylines will be $|A| \times |B| \times |C| = 27$. Each node of the expansion tree corresponds to a MEP. In particular, the root node (referred to as r or n_1) corresponds to MEP_1, i.e., the MEP that is formed by the top SEPs from each SEP skyline. MEP_1 has the smallest *score*

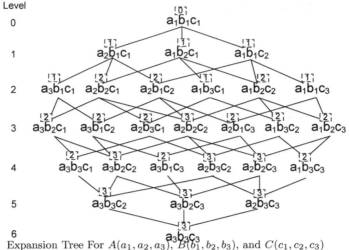

Fig. 5.1 Expansion Tree For $A(a_1, a_2, a_3)$, $B(b_1, b_2, b_3)$, and $C(c_1, c_2, c_3)$

and thus must belong to the skyline. A child node is different from a parent node by only one SEP and the SEP from the child node is the successor of the SEP from the parent in the corresponding SEP skyline.

We use the expansion tree $\mathcal{T}$ together with a heap $\mathcal{H}$ to achieve the basic progressive enumeration. Specifically, the expansion tree ensures that a parent node is enumerated before its child nodes. This is desirable because the *score* of a parent node cannot be larger than those from its children. The heap, on the other hand, determines the enumeration order of nodes that do not have a parent-child relationship. The enumeration starts by initializing the heap $\mathcal{H}$ with MEP_1 (i.e., n_1). Each enumeration step consists of two sub-steps: (1) **Extract**—the MEP with the smallest *score*, say n_i, is extracted from $\mathcal{H}$ and compared with the existing skyline. n_i will be inserted into the skyline if not dominated and discarded if otherwise. (2) **Expand**—the child nodes of n_i are then generated and inserted into $\mathcal{H}$. The enumeration stops when $\mathcal{H}$ is empty.

5.3.2 Node Duplication

A major issue with the above basic implementation is that a single node could be generated from parent expansion for multiple times, referred to as *node duplication*. This is because that a node could have up to m parents, where m is the number of SEP skylines. The same child node will be generated when each of its parents is expanded. As shown in Figure 5.1, the number above each node indicates the number of its parents. For example, the node (a_2, b_2, c_2) will be inserted into $\mathcal{H}$ for three times because it has three parents and when each of them is expanded, (a_2, b_2, c_2) will be generated and inserted into $\mathcal{H}$. The node duplication issue introduces great computational overhead because lots of node are processed multiple times. More seriously, the same node could be inserted into the skyline for more than one time, which results in a wrong skyline.

A straightforward extension to tackle the above issue is to add a *Parent Checking* (PC) procedure before inserting a node into the heap. For a given node, say n_i, generated from the expansion, PC examines whether there is any of its parents currently in the heap. If this is the case, the child will not be inserted. However, PC still cannot completely resolve the above issue. We use a specific example to explain this. With the expansion tree shown in Figure 5.1, nodes $(a_2, b_1, c_1), (a_1, b_2, c_1)$, and (a_1, b_1, c_2) will be generated and inserted into $\mathcal{H}$ after (a_1, b_1, c_1) is expanded. Assume that (a_2, b_1, c_1) has the smallest *score* so that it will be extracted from $\mathcal{H}$. After (a_2, b_1, c_1) is expanded, its three child nodes $(a_3, b_1, c_1), (a_2, b_2, c_1)$, and (a_2, b_1, c_2) are generated. With the checking procedure, only (a_3, b_1, c_1) is inserted into $\mathcal{H}$ because the parents of (a_2, b_2, c_1), and (a_2, b_1, c_2) are still in $\mathcal{H}$. Assume that (a_3, b_1, c_1) has the smallest *score* at this point. It is then extracted from $\mathcal{H}$ and expanded to generate its two child nodes (a_3, b_2, c_1) and (a_3, b_1, c_2). With the checking procedure, both (a_3, b_2, c_1) and (a_3, b_1, c_2) are inserted into $\mathcal{H}$ since none of their parents are in the heap. This is problematic because (a_3, b_2, c_1) and (a_3, b_1, c_2) are placed into the heap before some of their parents, i.e., (a_2, b_2, c_1), and (a_2, b_1, c_2). In this case, when the parent nodes are expanded, (a_3, b_2, c_1) and (a_3, b_1, c_2) will be generated again, respectively. This, again, results in node duplication.

The above analysis reveals that in order to completely avoid node duplication, we should check whether there is any ancestor (instead of only parent) of a node currently in the heap, i.e., as long as any ancestor of a node is still in the heap, the node will not be inserted into the heap. In the above example, (a_3, b_2, c_1) and (a_3, b_1, c_2) will not be inserted into $\mathcal{H}$ with ancestor checking because their ancestors (a_1, b_2, c_1) and (a_1, b_1, c_2) are in the heap. Node n_j, represented as $(\text{SEP}_{1j},...,\text{SEP}_{mj})$ is an ancestor of node n_i, represented as $(\text{SEP}_{1i},...,\text{SEP}_{mi})$ if $\text{SEP}_{kj}.\text{score} \leq \text{SEP}_{ki}.\text{score}, 1 \leq \forall k \leq m$. Therefore, the complexity of checking an ancestor relationship is $\Theta(m)$. For each node, the entire $\mathcal{H}$ needs to be checked. Thus, ancestor checking for a node requires a complexity of $\Theta(|\mathcal{H}| \times m)$, where $|\mathcal{H}|$ is the length of the heap at the point when the checking is conducted. Since a node will be generated when each of its parent is expanded, the overall complexity of ancestor checking for each node is $\Theta(|\mathcal{H}| \times m \times p)$, where p is the number of parents for the node. This is expensive especially when the size of $\mathcal{H}$ becomes large with the increase of the number of services (refer to Sect. 6.3.6 for details).

5.3.3 Parent Table

We introduce the *parent table* data structure in this section. The parent table provides a decent solution to tackle the node duplication issue with minimum overhead. Instead of keeping track of all the ancestors, the parent table only stores the information related to the number of parents for a given node. The underlying principle is that *a node can be inserted into the heap only after all its parents have been processed*. Since the maximum number of parents for a node is m, with m as the number of SEP skylines, the parent table only uses up to $(\lfloor \log m \rfloor + 1)$ bits for a given node. Now the question is how to decide the number of parents for a node. Based on the expansion tree, we have the following property.

Property 5.2. Assume that the index of each SEP skyline starts with 1. The number of parents for a given node n_i, represented as $(\text{SEP}_{1i}, ..., \text{SEP}_{mi})$, equals to the number of SEPs with an index greater than 1.   ■

Figure 5.1 shows the number of parents for each node in the expansion tree. With the parent table, the progressive enumeration now works as follows. The parent table, referred to as $\mathcal{P}$, is first initialized by setting each node entry as the number of parents for the node (refer to Property 5.2). Similar to the basic implementation, the heap $\mathcal{H}$ is initialized with the root of the expansion tree $\mathcal{T}$. Each enumeration step now consists of three substeps. The **Extract** and **Expand** are the same as before except that **Expand** only generates the child nodes and does not insert any of them into $\mathcal{H}$. A new **UpdateCheck** step is added, which works as follows. For each newly generated child node, it first updates $\mathcal{P}$ by subtracting 1 from the corresponding node entry. The updated entry now represents the remaining parent nodes that have not been processed yet. It then checks the entry. If the entry becomes 0, the corresponding node will be inserted into $\mathcal{H}$. By doing this, we make sure that a child node can only be inserted into the heap after all its parent nodes have been processed. Each **UpdateCheck** takes a complexity of $\Theta(1)$. Thus, for a node that has p parents, the overall overhead is $\Theta(p)$. The detailed progressive enumeration algorithm (referred to as *PEN*) is given in Algorithm 9.

Algorithm 9 _Progressive ENumeration (PEN)_

Require: m SEP skylines that form an expansion tree $\mathcal{T}$
Ensure: The MEP skyline $\mathcal{MS}$
 1: $\mathcal{MS} = \phi, \mathcal{H} = \phi$;
 2: Initialize the parent table $\mathcal{P}$;
 3: **while** $\mathcal{H} \neq \phi$ **do**
 4:     remove the top node n from $\mathcal{H}$;
 5:     **if** n is not dominated by $\mathcal{MS}$ **then**
 6:         $\mathcal{MS}.add(n)$;
 7:     **end if**
 8:     $\mathcal{CN} = \text{expand}(n, \mathcal{T})$; {generate the child nodes}
 9:     **for all** node $n_i \in \mathcal{CN}$ **do**
10:         $\mathcal{P}(n_i) = \mathcal{P}(n_i) - 1$;
11:         **if** $\mathcal{P}(n_i) == 0$ **then**
12:             $\mathcal{H}.add(n_i)$;
13:         **end if**
14:     **end for**
15: **end while**

Example 5.3. We use an example as shown in Figure 5.2 to explain the progressive enumeration process. Figure 5.2 (c) shows the enumeration steps with Figure 5.2 (d) and (e) illustrating the contents of the parent table and the heap, respectively. In step 1, (a_1, b_1) is removed from the heap and expanded to (a_2, b_1) and (a_1, b_2). For each of these two nodes, the corresponding entries in the parent table are first updated, i.e., $\mathcal{P}(a_1, b_2) = \mathcal{P}(a_1, b_2) - 1 = 0, \mathcal{P}(a_2, b_1) = \mathcal{P}(a_2, b_1) - 1 = 0$. Since both entries become 0 after the update, (a_2, b_1) and (a_1, b_2) are inserted into the heap. In step 2, (a_1, b_2) will be removed from the heap since it has the smallest score. It is expanded to $MEP(a_2, b_2)$ and $MEP(a_1, b_3)$. The parent table is updated as follows: $\mathcal{P}(a_2, b_2) = \mathcal{P}(a_2, b_2) - 1 = 1, \mathcal{P}(a_3, b_1) = \mathcal{P}(a_3, b_1) - 1 = 0$. Thus, only $MEP(a_1, b_3)$ is inserted into the heap. Figure 5.2 (c) shows the expansion direction of each step and a mark "$\times$" on the lines means that the generated node will not be inserted into the heap at that step (due to a nonzero parent entry). The entire enumeration stops when the heap becomes empty. ∎

5.3.4 Analysis

In what follows, we identify some key properties of _PEN_ and present the proof of correctness. We then investigate the overall complexity of DPA.

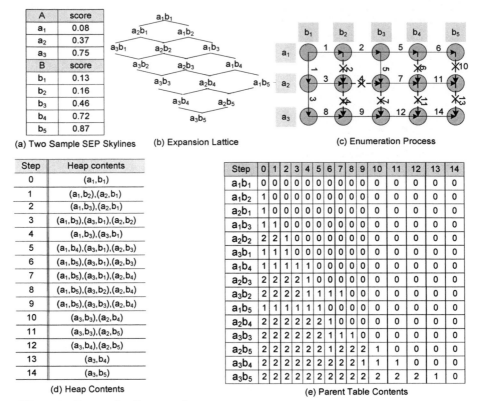

(a) Two Sample SEP Skylines

A	score
a_1	0.08
a_2	0.37
a_3	0.75
B	score
b_1	0.13
b_2	0.16
b_3	0.46
b_4	0.72
b_5	0.87

(b) Expansion Lattice

(c) Enumeration Process

(d) Heap Contents

Step	Heap contents
0	(a_1,b_1)
1	$(a_1,b_2),(a_2,b_1)$
2	$(a_1,b_3),(a_2,b_1)$
3	$(a_1,b_3),(a_3,b_1),(a_2,b_2)$
4	$(a_1,b_3),(a_3,b_1)$
5	$(a_1,b_4),(a_3,b_1),(a_2,b_3)$
6	$(a_1,b_5),(a_3,b_1),(a_2,b_3)$
7	$(a_1,b_5),(a_3,b_1),(a_2,b_4)$
8	$(a_1,b_5),(a_3,b_2),(a_2,b_4)$
9	$(a_1,b_5),(a_3,b_3),(a_2,b_4)$
10	$(a_3,b_3),(a_2,b_4)$
11	$(a_3,b_3),(a_2,b_5)$
12	$(a_3,b_4),(a_2,b_5)$
13	(a_3,b_4)
14	(a_3,b_5)

(e) Parent Table Contents

Step	0	1	2	3	4	5	6	7	8	9	10	11	12	13	14
a_1b_1	0	0	0	0	0	0	0	0	0	0	0	0	0	0	0
a_1b_2	1	0	0	0	0	0	0	0	0	0	0	0	0	0	0
a_2b_1	1	0	0	0	0	0	0	0	0	0	0	0	0	0	0
a_1b_3	1	1	0	0	0	0	0	0	0	0	0	0	0	0	0
a_2b_2	2	2	1	0	0	0	0	0	0	0	0	0	0	0	0
a_3b_1	1	1	1	1	0	0	0	0	0	0	0	0	0	0	0
a_1b_4	1	1	1	1	1	0	0	0	0	0	0	0	0	0	0
a_2b_3	2	2	2	2	1	0	0	0	0	0	0	0	0	0	0
a_3b_2	2	2	2	2	1	1	1	1	0	0	0	0	0	0	0
a_1b_5	1	1	1	1	1	1	0	0	0	0	0	0	0	0	0
a_2b_4	2	2	2	2	2	2	1	0	0	0	0	0	0	0	0
a_3b_3	2	2	2	2	2	2	1	1	1	0	0	0	0	0	0
a_2b_5	2	2	2	2	2	2	1	2	2	2	1	0	0	0	0
a_3b_4	2	2	2	2	2	2	2	2	2	1	1	1	0	0	0
a_3b_5	2	2	2	2	2	2	2	2	2	2	2	2	2	1	0

Fig. 5.2   Progressive Enumeration

5.3.4.1 Correctness

Lemma 5.4. *PEN processes the nodes (i.e.,MEPs) in an ascending order of their scores.*

PROOF: Assume that we have n_i processed earlier than n_j whereas $score(n_j) < score(n_i)$. Assume that at a certain point, n_i becomes the node that has the smallest *score* in the heap. Thus, n_j cannot be in the heap because otherwise n_j should have the smallest *score*. Since n_j has not been processed at that point, it must not be inserted into the heap yet. Thus, we can always find a node n_k currently in the heap, which is an ancestor of n_j. Extracting n_k from the heap will (directly or indirectly) trigger the insertion of n_j into the heap. Now, we have two cases to deal with: (1) $n_i = n_k$; and (2) $n_i \neq n_k$. Case (1) means that n_i is an ancestor of n_j, which contradicts that n_i has a larger *score* than that of n_j. For case (2), we have $score(n_i) < score(n_k)$ and $score(n_k) \leq score(n_j)$. Thus, we have $score(n_i) < score(n_j)$, which leads to a contradiction. ∎

Lemma 5.5. *Every node will be examined by PEN.*

PROOF: Suppose that there is a set of nodes, S, that is ignored by *PEN*, where $S \neq \phi$. We can always choose a node say, $n = (a_i, b_j, c_k, ...)$, such that there does not exist a node $n' = (a'_i, b'_j, c'_k...)$ in S satisfying that $i' \leq i \wedge j' \leq j \wedge k' \leq k....$ Since n is ignored by *PEN*, we can conclude that each time when one of its parents is processed, the remaining parent number is always larger than 0 (according to Algorithm 9). It means that at least one parent of n is ignored by *PEN*, too. This contradicts the selection of node n. ∎

5.3.4.2 Complexity

Lemma 5.4 and Lemma 5.5 collectively ensure the correctness of DPA. We investigate the performance of DPA by examining the cost on each node in the expansion tree. The time spent by DPA on node n_i consists of two major parts: heap operation (i.e., insertion and extraction) and skyline comparison. Assume that the size of the MEP space is $\mathcal{N}$ and expected size of the MEP skyline $\mathcal{MS}$ is $\Theta((\ln^{d-1} \mathcal{N})/(d-1)!)$ [37]. The number of comparisons between skyline MEPs is $|\mathcal{MS}|^2/2$, which is $o(\mathcal{N})$. Since the MEP space is examined in a sorted order, the number of comparisons between skyline MEPs and non-skyline MEPs is bounded by $O(\mathcal{N})$ [37]. The cost of heap operation is determined by the size of the heap, which we examine in detail in the remaining part of this section.

Lemma 5.6. *A node and its ancestors (or descendants) cannot coexist in the heap.*
PROOF: Assume that we have both n_i and one of its ancestor n_j in the heap at a certain point. n_j cannot be the parent of n_i because when n_i is inserted into the heap, all its parents must already have been extracted from the heap. In this case, n_j should be the ancestor of one of n_i's parent, say n_k. Similarly, n_j cannot be the parent of n_k because otherwise n_j will be extracted from the heap before n_k. Following this, we will have two situations: (1) n_j coincides with the root r of the expansion tree; or (2) n_j does not exist (when n_j is a non-parent ancestor of n_k which is a child node of the root). Case (2) directly contradicts the assumption. Case (1) also leads to a contradiction because r is extracted from the heap in the very beginning of *PEN*. ∎

The order between the nodes that are incomparable (i.e., nodes that do not have a ancestor-successor relationship) with the expansion tree is decided by the heap. Therefore, *the upper bound of the heap size is determined by the maximum number of incomparable nodes that can concurrently reside in the heap*. Some important properties of the expansion tree helps provide an answer for this. For the ease of analysis, we assume that the index for each SEP skyline starts from 0 and the size of each SEP skyline is $(k+1)$. Thus, the index range for the jth SEP skyline is $0 \leq i_j \leq k$. Assume that there are m SEP skylines and the level number of the expansion tree stats with 0.

With the above settings, we can immediately derive the number of nodes in each level of the expansion tree. Based on how the expansion tree is constructed (refer to Sect. 5.3.1 for details), the indices of the SEPs within a given node sum to the level number, upon which the node resides. Thus, for any node $(SEP_{i_1}, SEP_{i_2}, ..., SEP_{i_m})$ on level l, we have $i_1 + i_2 + \cdots + i_m = l$. As can be seen from Figure 5.1, after subtracting 1 from each index of a given node (because the index here starts from 1 instead of 0), the sum of the indices equals to the corresponding level number. Therefore, the number of nodes on a given level is actually the number of integral solutions of $i_1 + i_2 + \cdots + i_m = l, 0 \leq i_j \leq k$. This is given by the following equation:

$$N_l(m, k) = \sum_{j=0}^{[l/(k+1)]} (-1)^j \binom{m}{j} \binom{l + m - 1 - j(k+1)}{m - 1} \tag{5.1}$$

where $[l/(k+1)]$ is the integer part of $l/(k+1)$. Eq. (5.1) has also been used in combinatorial analysis [69]. Another way to interpret this is that $N_l(m, k)$ is the coefficient of x^l in the expansion of $(1 + x + \cdots + x^k)^m$. $N_l(m, k)$ achieves its maximum value at the middle level of the expansion tree [21], i.e.,

$$\max(\{N_l(m, k) | 0 \leq l \leq mk\}) = N_{[\frac{mk}{2}]}(m, k) \tag{5.2}$$

The expansion tree has a symmetrical structure, which can be justified by the following lemma.

Lemma 5.7. *The lth level and the $(mk - l)$th level of the expansion tree have the same number of nodes i.e., $N_l(m, k) = N_{mk-l}(m, k)$.*
PROOF: The number of nodes on level l is determined by the number of integral solutions of $i_1 + i_2 + \cdots + i_m = l, 0 \leq i_j \leq k$. Suppose that $i_j = k - t_j, 1 \leq j \leq m$. Thus, we have

$$(k - t_1) + (k - t_2) + \cdots + (k - t_m) = l, 0 \leq t_j \leq k \tag{5.3}$$
$$\Rightarrow t_1 + t_2 + \cdots + t_m = mk - l, 0 \leq t_j \leq k \tag{5.4}$$

Since there is a one-to-one correspondence relationship between i_j and t_j, the number of integral solutions of $i_1 + i_2 + \cdots + i_m = l, 0 \leq i_j \leq k$ equals to the number of integral solutions of $t_1 + t_2 + \cdots + t_m = mk - l, 0 \leq t_j \leq k$, which determines the number of nodes on level $mk - l$. ∎

Lemma 5.8. *The nodes on the same level of the expansion tree are not comparable to each other.*
PROOF: This is straightforward because the nodes on the same level do not hold an ancestor-successor relationship. ∎

Theorem 5.9. *The size of the heap $\mathcal{H}$ is bounded by the number of nodes on the middle level of the expansion tree, i.e., $\max(|\mathcal{H}|) = N_{[\frac{mk}{2}]}(m, k)$.*
PROOF: This actually means that the upper bound of the heap is achieved when all the nodes on the middle level of the expansion tree concurrently

reside in the heap. To prove this, we assume that the maximum size of the heap is achieved when there are nodes from some levels above the middle (same conclusion can be drawn for the levels below the middle due to symmetrical property stated in Lemma 5.7). Assume that n_i is from level i, where $i < \lceil \frac{mk}{2} \rceil$. All the nodes in the heap cannot be the successor of n_i. Suppose n_i is expanded at this point. Therefore, all its m child nodes can be inserted into the heap, with $m > 1$. This contradicts that the heap has already achieved its maximum size before n_i is expanded. ∎

We now asymptotically investigate the heap size based on Eq. (5.1). This provides an intuitive way to understand how heap size increases with some key parameters, including the size of the individual SEP skylines (i.e., k) and the number of services (i.e., m). Specifically, let $l = pk$, where $0 \leq p \leq m$, and we have,

$$
\binom{l + m - 1 - j(k + 1)}{m - 1} = \binom{(p - j)k - j + (m - 1)}{m - 1}
$$
$$
= \frac{1}{(m - 1)!} \times ((p - j)k - j + (m - 1))
$$
$$
\times ((p - j)k - j + (m - 2))
$$
$$
\cdots
$$
$$
\times ((p - j)k - j + (1))
$$

On the right hand side, the product multiplies $(m - 1)$ items in addition to $\frac{1}{(m-1)!}$, where each of these $(m - 1)$ items contains $(p - j)k$. This allows us to rewrite the right hand side as the $(m - 1)$ powers of k,

$$
\binom{l + m - 1 - j(k + 1)}{m - 1} = \frac{(p - j)^{m-1}}{(m - 1)!} k^{m-1} + \Theta(k^{m-2}) \qquad (5.5)
$$

The remaining terms can be expressed as $\Theta(k^{m-2})$ because the number of SEP skylines (i.e., the number of services) is expected to be much less than the size of the SEP skyline, i.e., $m \ll k$. We also have $j \leq \lceil \frac{l}{k+1} \rceil \leq m \ll k$. Therefore, the magnitude of the remaining terms is dominated by the highest power of k, which is $(m - 2)$. Based on Eq. (5.5), Eq. (5.1) can be rewritten as

$$
N_l(m, k) = \frac{\sum_{j=0}^{\lceil l/(k+1) \rceil} (-1)^j \binom{m}{j} (p - j)^{m-1}}{(m - 1)!} k^{m-1} + \Theta(k^{m-2}) \qquad (5.6)
$$

Eq. (5.6) shows that the heap size increases exponentially with the number of services although it may have a small constant factor. Also, the upper bound of the heap size cannot exceed k^{m-1}. This can be illustrated in a more intuitive manner. Assume that at certain point, the size of the heap exceeds k^{m-1}. In this case, we must have at least two nodes that are different from each other by only one SEP. Suppose that these two nodes are $(s_{1i},...,s_{jx},...,s_{mi})$ (referred to n_x) and $(s_{1i},...,s_{jy},...,s_{mi})$ (referred to as n_y), respectively, where $x \neq y$. Therefore, n_x is a ancestor (or a descendant) of n_y. The coexistence of n_x and n_y contradicts with Lemma 5.6.

Assume that the heap size is $|\mathcal{H}^{in}(n_i)|$ (or $|\mathcal{H}^{out}(n_i)|$) when node n_i is inserted into (or removed from) the heap. Then, the cost for inserting n_i into $\mathcal{H}$ is $\log(|\mathcal{H}^{in}(n_i)|)$. Although the cost for heap extraction is a constant, a reorganization of the heap is required after n_i is extracted, which has a cost of $\log(|\mathcal{H}^{out}(n_i)|)$. Since the total number of nodes in the expansion tree is $\mathcal{N}$, the overall cost of heap operations is

$$\sum_{i=1}^{\mathcal{N}}[\log(|\mathcal{H}^{in}(n_i)|) + \log(|\mathcal{H}^{out}(n_i)|)] \tag{5.7}$$

Since the cost for skyline comparison is $O(\mathcal{N})$, the overall complexity of DPA is dominated by Eq. (5.7).

5.4 A Bottom-Up Approach

The DPA algorithm is able to progressively report the MEP skyline. As shown in Sect. 6.3.6, its performance is decided by the size of MEP space and the heap size. With the increment of the number of services, the total number of MEPs will increase in an exponential manner. Similarly, the upper bound of the heap also grows exponentially due to Theorem 5.9. In this case, although DPA can still efficiently report an initial answer set (due to the progressiveness), its performance to compute the entire skyline remains to be an issue especially for a large number of services. In this section, we present a bottom-up approach to efficiently compute the entire MEP skyline while keeping all the nice properties (i.e., progressive and pipelineable) of DPA.

5.4.1 The Early Pruning Heuristic

As discussed in Sect. 6.3.6, the performance of DPA is decided by two factors: the size of the MEP space (i.e., $\mathcal{N}$) and the heap size (i.e., $|\mathcal{H}|$). The bottom-up approach is built based upon DPA. It leverages an *Early Pruning* (EP) heuristic to reduce both of these two factors in computing the skyline. We first present a key observation which grounds the EP heuristic.

Theorem 5.10. *If MEP $n_i^{(m+1)}$, represented as $(SEP_{1i}, ..., SEP_{(m+1)i})$ belongs to the $(m + 1)$-MEP skyline (i.e., the skyline computed over $(m + 1)$*

services), then MEP $n_i^{(m)}$, represented as $(SEP_{1i}, ..., SEP_{mi})$, must belong to the m-MEP skyline.

PROOF: Assume that $n_i^{(m)}$ is not in the m MEP skyline. Thus, we can always find a $n_j^{(m)}$ such that $n_j^{(m)} \rhd n_i^{(m)}$. By combining $n_j^{(m)}$ with $\text{SEP}_{(m+1)i}$, we have $(n_j^{(m)}, \text{SEP}_{(m+1)i}) \rhd (n_i^{(m)}, \text{SEP}_{(m+1)i})$, which contradicts that $n_i^{(m+1)}$ is in the skyline.   ■

Theorem 5.10 implies that if $n_i^{(m)} \notin$ m-MEP skyline, then $n_i^{(m)}$ cannot be part of any MEP in the $(m+1)$-MEP skyline. Thus, we can safely prune $n_i^{(m)}$ when computing the m-MEP skyline. This actually has the effect of pruning k MEPs in the $(m+1)$-MEP space, where k is the size of the $(m+1)$th SEP skyline. The bottom-up approach is built upon this EP heuristic. *Instead of considering all the m services simultaneously (as DPA), it progressively combines the m services together.* Specifically, it combines $m'(m' < m)$ SEP (or intermediate MEP) skylines by using DPA in each step and keeps doing this until m is reached. Since DPA is completely pipelineable and the generated skyline MEPs are automatically sorted, a skyline MEP can be immediately used for the next-phase skyline computation. This guarantees the progressiveness of the bottom-up approach. There are two remaining questions: (Q_1) *how to choose m'*, and (Q_2) *in what order to combine the temporary skylines.* The selection of m' is straightforward due to Theorem 5.10. To achieve the maximum pruning efficiency of EP, we should always compute the skyline from the minimum number of SEP (or intermediate MEP) skylines in each step, i.e., we choose $m' = 2$.

5.4.2 Linear Composition Plans

For (Q_2), we first use an example to illustrate what it actually implies. We then present our solution for it. Figure 5.3 shows two different ways to combine the SEP and intermediate MEP skylines, which we refer to as *composition plans*. Figure 5.3(a) gives a linear composition plan, where at least one child of a composition node is an SEP skyline. On the other hand, a nonlinear or a bushy plan is shown in Figure 5.3(b). The following lemma helps us determine which type of plan to use.

Lemma 5.11. *The heap size used by DPA to compose two skylines X and Y has an upper bound of $min(|X|, |Y|)$.*
PROOF: For any two MEPs in the heap, say n_s represented as (x_{is}, y_{js}) and n_t represented as (x_{it}, y_{jt}), $x_{is} \neq x_{it}$ and $y_{js} \neq y_{jt}$. Suppose $|X| < |Y|$. We assume there are $|X| + 1$ MEPs in the heap. Therefore, there must exist two MEPs that share the same entry from X. This contradicts Lemma 5.6.   ■

Assume that the sizes of the SEP skylines are all around k. Thus, a linear composition plan guarantees that the cost of any individual heap operation

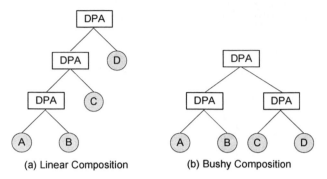

(a) Linear Composition   (b) Bushy Composition

Fig. 5.3   Composition Plans

during the entire skyline computation is bounded by $\log(k)$. In contrast, in a bushy plan, the cost of the heap operations are determined by the sizes of the intermediate MEP skylines. In addition, since the size of the intermediate MEP skyline is typically larger than any of its children (we analyze this below), the cost of heap operations will keep increasing, which may become rather significant especially for a large number of services. On the other hand, the cost of heap operations for a linear plan is insensitive to the number of services, which helps it achieve a much better scalability.

The only remaining question now is to justify that the size of the intermediate MEP skyline (referred to as $S_{(i,j)}$) is indeed larger than any of its two children (referred to as S_i and S_j respectively). A straightforward way is to use the skyline cardinality estimation approach presented in [25], where we assume that the size of $S_{(i,j)}$ takes the form of $K_1 \log^{K_2}(|S_i| \times |S_j|)$ and parameters K_1 and K_2 can be estimated based on small data samples. Here, we present a more intuitive approach to roughly estimate the size of a intermediate MEP skyline. Suppose that we want to compose two skylines A and B. The sizes of B and A are k and k', respectively. Skyline A consists of a_1, a_2, a_3, and a_4, as shown in Figure 5.4(a). For skyline B, instead of highlighting each individual skyline point, we use a curve to approximate the overall distribution of the skyline points for the ease of analysis. For the composition of A and B, we first compose each skyline point in A with B and then combine the result together. For example, for composing a_1 and B, we only need to shift the skyline curve of B with a distance of $a_1[x]$ along the x axis and a distance of $a_1[y]$ along the y axis. Figure 5.4(b) shows the obtained result lists of composing a_1, a_2 and a_3 with B. Each result list is sorted based on the x values. We assume that there is a crossing point for every two consecutive compositions. For example, $a_1 + B$ and $a_2 + B$ cross at (x_1, y_1). (x_1, y_1) coincides with two virtual points [1] $(b_{21}[x] + a_1[x], b_{21}[y] + a_1[y])$ and $(b_{21}[x] + a_1[x], b_{21}[y] + a_1[y])$, that are from $a_1 + B$ and $a_2 + B$ respectively. Since $a_2[x] > a_1[x]$, we have $b_{12}[x] > b_{21}[x]$. Thus, we have $k_{12} > k_{21}$ (be-

---

[1] We call them virtual because there may be no actual points in the results list that corresponds to (x_1, y_1).

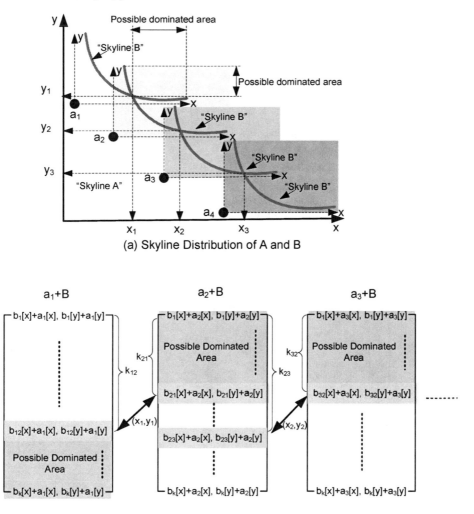

(a) Skyline Distribution of A and B

(b) Cardinality Esitmation

Fig. 5.4 Cardinality Estimation for Intermediate Skylines

cause the list is sorted on x). We generously assume that the points lay in the "possible dominated areas" (i.e., the lower part of $a_1 + B$ and the upper part of $a_2 + B$, as shown in Figure 5.4(a)) are actually all dominated. Therefore, the remaining number of points is $(a_1, a_2, B) = k_{12} + (k - k_{21})$, which is greater than k because $k_{12} > k_{21}$. Similarly, we then combine $a_2 + B$ and $a_3 + B$ and have $(a_2, a_3, B) = (k_{23} - k_{21}) + (k - k_{32})$. We subtract k_{21} because these are dominated by $a_1 + B$. In addition, we keep the term $(k_{23} - k_{21})$ only if $k_{23} > k_{21}$, otherwise, $(a_2, a_3, B) = (k - k_{32})$. We keep applying this and obtain the final size of the skyline as $K_{AB} = \sum_{i=1}^{k'-1}(a_i, a_{i+1}, B)$. We have

$K_{AB} > \max(k, k')$ because $(a_1, a_2, B) \geq (k+1)$ and all the remaining $(k'-2)$ items are greater than or equal to 1.

5.4.3 Complexity Analysis

Similar to our previous analysis, we assume without loss of generality that there are m services and the sizes of the SEP skylines are around k. The bottom-up approach employs $(m-1)$ phases to compute the m-MEP skyline. We use the notion $k_{(i+1)}$ to represent the size of the MEP skyline generated from phase i. To adapt to this notion, we have $k_{(1)} = k$. For phase i, the complexity can be expressed as follows:

$$\underbrace{2 \times k \times k_{(i)} \times \log k}_{\text{heap operation}} + \underbrace{k \times k_{(i)} + \frac{1}{2} k_{(i+1)}^2}_{\text{skyline comparison}} \tag{5.8}$$

Thus, we have the overall complexity as

$$\sum_{i=1}^{m-1} 2 \times k \times k_{(i)} \times \log k + k \times k_{(i)} + \frac{1}{2} k_{(i+1)}^2 \tag{5.9}$$

$$= k(2 \log k + 1) \sum_{i=1}^{m-1} k_{(i)} + \frac{1}{2} \sum_{i=1}^{m-1} k_{(i+1)}^2 \tag{5.10}$$

Based on the above analysis on the intermediate skyline size, we have $k_{(i)} < k_{(i+1)} < k \times k_{(i)}$. Thus,

$$\frac{1}{k} < \frac{k_{(i)}}{k_{(i+1)}} < 1 \tag{5.11}$$

Assume

$$\max\left(\frac{k_{(i)}}{k_{(i+1)}}\right) = \frac{1}{p}, 1 \leq \forall i \leq m-1 \text{ and } 1 < p < k \tag{5.12}$$

Therefore, we have

$$\sum_{i=1}^{m-1} k_{(i)} < \frac{1}{1 - \frac{1}{p}} \times k_{(i)} = \frac{p}{p-1} k_{(m-1)} \tag{5.13}$$

$$\sum_{i=1}^{m-1} k_{(i+1)}^2 < \frac{1}{1 - \frac{1}{p^2}} \times k_{(i+1)} = \frac{p^2}{p^2 - 1} k_{(m)}^2 \tag{5.14}$$

Since we have $k_{(m)} > k_{(m-1)} > k$ and also note that $k_{(m)} = |\mathcal{MS}|$, the overall complexity can be derived as $O(\frac{p^2}{2(p^2-1)}|\mathcal{MS}|^2)$. This is nearly optimal because to compute a skyline with size $|\mathcal{MS}|$, at least $|\mathcal{MS}|^2/2$ skyline to skyline comparisons are required.

5.5 Experimental Study

We implement all the proposed algorithms: OPA, DPA, and BUA. We conduct an extensive set of experiments to assess the performance of these algorithms. We run our experiments on a cluster of *Sun Enterprise Ultra 10* workstations with 512 Mbytes Ram under *Solaris* operating system. The QoWS attributes of service instances are generated in three different ways following the approach described in [14]: 1) *Independent QoWS* where all the QoWS attributes of service instances are uniformly distributed, 2) *Anti-correlated QoWS* where a service instance is good at one of the QoWS attributes but bad in one or all of the other QoWS attributes, and 3) *Correlated QoWS* where a service instance which is good at one of the QoWS attributes is also good at the other QoWS attributes. We build indices on the SEP space (refer to Chapter 4) and use BBS [60] to compute the SEP skylines. Thus, the SEP skylines are automatically sorted based on the scores of their SEPs. Table 5.2 gives the parameter settings of the experiments.

Table 5.2 Experiment Parameters

Parameter	Description	Value
n	Cardinality of service relations	100k
d	Number of QoWS attributes	[2,5]
m	Number of Services	[2,10]

5.5.1 Efficiency and Scalability

We evaluate the performance in terms of total CPU cost against d and m in this section. It is worth to note that the sizes of the SEP skylines keep increasing with d, which is especially obvious with the anti-correlated QoWS. For instance, the size of a SEP skylines typically exceeds 1000 when $d \geq 5$. In practice, a service query may typically pose some other quality constraints, which help prune a large portion of the SEP skyline. To avoid overly large SEP skylines, we select the top 100 skyline SEPs (based on their scores) from them. Under this setting, the candidate MEP space $\mathcal{N}$ can still become very large with the increase of the number of services, for example, $\mathcal{N} = 10^{20}$, when $m = 10$.

Figure 5.5 compares the three algorithms, BUA, DPA, and OPA with $m = 4$ and $d \in [2, 5]$. When $d = 2$, which also corresponds to a relatively small candidate MEP space, OPA performs slightly more efficiently than BUA because it requires no overhead to maintain progressiveness. It also benefits from the effectiveness of the `EnumerateNext` function. BUA performs the most efficiently for all other cases. In particular, the performance advantage of BUA over the other two algorithms becomes larger as d increases. It is also interesting that the CPU cost of DPA does not necessarily increase with d for independent and correlated QoWS. This is because the performance of DPA is decided by both the size of the MEP space $\mathcal{N}$ and the heap size $|\mathcal{H}|$. For anti-correlated QoWS, the sizes of the SEP skylines increase quickly with d. This results in a large $\mathcal{N}$, which make it a dominating factor in the overall cost. In contrast, for independent and correlated QoWS, the increasing speed on sizes of the SEP skylines is typically much slower, which makes $|\mathcal{H}|$ play an important role in the overall cost. Since $|\mathcal{H}|$ may not necessarily increase with d (as shown in Figure 5.7), the overall CPU cost of DPA does not necessarily increase with d for independent and correlated QoWS.

Figure 5.6 evaluates the impact of m. Both DPA and OPA fail to output the skyline within reasonable time for $m > 4$ ($m > 5$) on anti-correlated and independent (correlated) QoWS. DPA is less efficient than OPA because the heap size $|\mathcal{H}|$ increases quickly with m. The result demonstrates that BUA is more efficient than the other two algorithms (with orders of magnitude) and can easily scale to a large number of services.

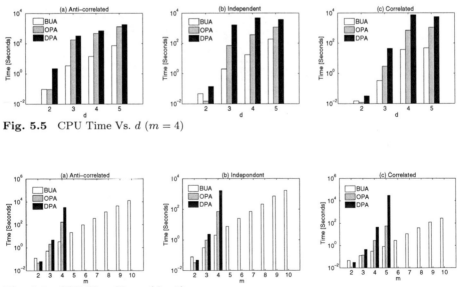

Fig. 5.5   CPU Time Vs. d ($m = 4$)

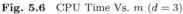

Fig. 5.6   CPU Time Vs. m ($d = 3$)

5.5.2 Heap Size

We evaluate how the maximum heap size changes with d and m in this section. As shown in Figure 5.7, the maximum heap sizes of BUA are smaller than those of DPA by several orders of magnitude with all $d \in [2, 5]$. Also, it is interesting to note that the maximum heap size does not necessarily increase with d for both DPA and BUA. For BUA, the maximum heap size is actually bounded by the maximum SEP skyline size, which is due to Lemma 5.11. For DPA, it is determined by the maximum number of incomparable MEPs that coincide in the heap. Although with the increase of d, the chance of incomparability between MEPs may increase as well, there are some other important factors that may affect the maximum heap size, such as the relative order of putting the MEPs in the heap.

Figure 5.8 evaluates the maximum heap size against m. The heap size of BUA is significantly less than that of DPA. The only exception is when $m = 2$, when BUA becomes identical to DPA. It is also important to note that the heap size of BUA is insensitive to m at all, which accounts for the good scalability of BUA. The maximum heap size of DPA, on the other hand, increases exponentially. The DPA heap goes beyond the size of main memory for $m > 4$ ($m > 5$) on anti-correlated and independent (correlated) QoWS.

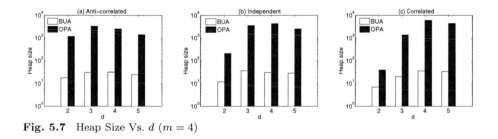

Fig. 5.7 Heap Size Vs. d ($m = 4$)

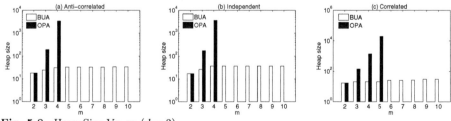

Fig. 5.8 Heap Size Vs. m ($d = 3$)

5.5.3 MEP Skyline Size

We evaluate the effect of the MEP skyline size in this section. Figure 5.9 shows that, in BUA, the MEP skyline size for i services (referred to as $k_{(i)}$) is greater than skyline size for $(i-1)$ services (referred to as $k_{(i-1)}$) and less than $k_i \times k_{(i-1)}$ for all $m \in [3, 10]$. This is consistent with our theoretical analysis on the intermediate skyline size, which is summarized as Eq. (5.11).

Figure 5.10 evaluates the effectiveness of the `EnumerateNext` function for OPA. The sizes of MEP skylines generally keep increasing over all iterations. The sizes only drop occasionally and slightly due to the removing of the false positives. Therefore, the `EnumerateNext` function effectively reduces the chances of generating false positive skyline MEPs, which accounts for efficient performance of OPA for generating the entire MEP skylines, especially for a small MEP space.

5.5.4 Discussion

Since OPA is more efficient than DPA, an interesting question is whether we can replace DPA with OPA in BUA. We choose DPA over OPA due to two major reasons. First, by using DPA, BUA is able to progressively report the MEP skyline. Second, the reason that OPA is more efficient than DPA is that it relies on the `EnumerateNext` function, whose effectiveness is built upon that the skylines are sorted. However, since the skylines generated by OPA is not sorted, we need to sort each intermediate skyline if using OPA with BUA, which will introduce significant overhead. In addition, a key reason that the performance of DPA degrades with m is due to the increase of the heap size. In BUA, we combine two skylines in each step and the heap size is invariant to m. In this case, DPA has a very similar performance with OPA (as shown in Figure 5.6 when $m = 2$).

We also investigate the situation when the sizes of the SEP skylines are significantly different from each other. We compute ten SEP skylines from anti-correlated, independent, and correlated QoWS and the ranges of their sizes are $[81, 162]$, $[57, 95]$, and $[28, 51]$, respectively. We explore three different orders to combine these skylines using BUA: sorted (based on their sizes), reversely sorted, and randomly ordered. As shown in Figure 5.11, the performances of the three composition orders are only slightly different from each other. A closer investigation reveals that the sorted order performs most inefficiently for all $m \in [5, 10]$. This is most obvious with the anti-correlaed QoWS. The major reason is as follows. Since the MEP skyline size keeps increasing with m, the overall cost of skyline computation is mainly affected by the cost of the last step. When a sorted order is adopted, the last SEP skyline has the largest size. This typically results in a large MEP space for the last step computation, which accounts for a high cost. Since the performance difference between reversely sorted order and random order is almost indistinguishable, we just need to avoid a sorted order if a further performance tuning is required for BUA.

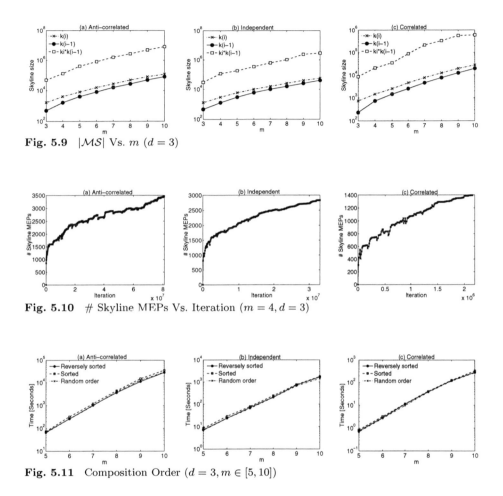

Fig. 5.9 $|\mathcal{MS}|$ Vs. m $(d = 3)$

Fig. 5.10 # Skyline MEPs Vs. Iteration $(m = 4, d = 3)$

Fig. 5.11 Composition Order $(d = 3, m \in [5, 10])$

Chapter 6
Skyline Computation over Uncertain QoWS

Quality of Web service (QoWS) has become a central criterion for differentiating competing service providers considering the increasing number of services with similar functionalities. The current service optimization paradigm assumes that precise QoWS values are available for selecting the competing service providers [94, 92]. Consider a Hotel Web service that provides hotel search and online reservation functionalities. Service users can locate hotels near their travel destinations and make the reservation via this service. Typically, there could be multiple service providers, $S_1,...,S_k$ (e.g., Holiday Inn, Days Inn, etc), competing with each other offering different user-centered quality. Quality attributes may include response time, fee, and reputation, etc. To select a satisfactory hotel, users usually need to go through a series of trial-run processes. If the number of competing providers is large, this would be very painstaking. Based on this example, the QoWS values of the provider S_i of the Hotel service could be: response time (2 seconds), fee (30 dollars), and reputation (2 stars). An objective function $\mathcal{F}(\mathbf{q}, \mathbf{w})$ is then defined, where $\mathbf{q}$ is the set of QoWS parameters and $\mathbf{w}$ is a set of weights assigned for each parameter in $\mathbf{q}$. The objective function $\mathcal{F}$ assigns a scalar value to each service provider and the provider gaining the highest value will be selected and returned to the user. However, there are two major limitations affiliated with the current service optimization approaches.

- First, current service optimization approaches require users to transform personal preferences into numeric weights. Users may not know enough to make tradeoffs between different quality aspects using numbers. Furthermore, most existing approaches work like a "black box", where users submit their weights over quality parameters and the system selected provider is returned. Users thus lose the flexibility to select their desired providers by themselves.
- Second, current service optimization approaches assume that the quality delivered by service providers do not change over time. In addition, the QoWS values are usually obtained from the corresponding service de-

Q. Yu and A. Bouguettaya, *Foundations for Efficient Web Service Selection*,
DOI 10.1007/978-1-4419-0314-3_6, © Springer Science+Business Media, LLC 2009

scriptions (referred to as tentative values) or computed by aggregating values over multiple transactions. However, these tentative or aggregated QoWS values may not precisely reflect the actual performance of a service provider. First, the performance of a service provider may fluctuate due to the dynamic service environment. For example, the response time may vary due the quality of the network and the fee for reserving a room may change with seasons. Second, service providers may not always deliver according to their "promised" quality because of "intentional" deceptions. Therefore, the actual QoWS delivered by service providers is inherently uncertain. Selecting service providers based on the tentative or aggregated QoWS values does not capture the inherent uncertainty of the actual QoWS.

Computing the skylines from service providers (referred to as *service skylines*) comes as a natural solution that overcomes the first limitation. Skyline computation has received significant consideration in database research [14, 80, 47, 60]. For a d-dimensional data set, the skyline consists of a set of points which are not dominated by any other points. A point $\mathbf{p}\ (p_1, ..., p_d)$ dominates another point $\mathbf{r}\ (r_1, ..., r_d)$ if $\forall\ i \in [1, d], p_i \succeq r_i$ and $\exists\ j \in [1, d], p_j \succ r_j$. We use $\succeq$ to generally represent *better than or equal to* and $\succ$ to represent *better than*. In the context of Web services, a service skyline can be regarded as a set of service providers that are not dominated by others in terms of all user interested QoWS attributes, such as response time, fee, and reputation. Computing service skylines can completely free users from assigning weights over different QoWS parameters. The skylines also guarantee that the user desired service providers are included so that users can make flexible selection from them.

To overcome the second limitation, we need to investigate a more challenging problem: *computing service skylines from uncertain QoWS*. We present in this chapter a novel concept, called *p-dominant service skyline* and a set of efficient algorithms to address the above issue. The remainder of this chapter is organized as follows. We present in Section 6.1 the concept of p-dominant service skyline and describe our contribution. We formally define the problem in Section 6.2 and illustrate the key difference between p-dominant skyline and p-skyline. We present the p-R-tree indexing structure and an two-phase algorithm to compute the p-dominant skyline in Section 6.3. We evaluate the efficiency and the effectiveness of the proposed new concepts, indexing structures, and algorithms through a comprehensive set of experimental study in Section 6.4.

6.1 p-dominant Service Skyline

We assume that the actual QoWS values delivered by a provider are available through a set of transaction logs obtained from some QoWS monitoring mechanisms [46, 7]. A transaction is modeled as a multi-dimensional data point, where each dimension corresponds to a QoWS attribute. Thus, the dominance relationship between transactions follows the standard semantics as described above.

Before introducing the p-dominant service skyline, we first use an example to illustrate the different implications for computing service skylines from certain and uncertain QoWS.

Example 6.1. Consider two providers S and T that offer the similar Hotel *Web service. The performance of S and T is recorded by a series of transaction logs, which help capture the actual QoWS delivered by each of these providers in practice. The dynamic environment, in which these providers operate, causes the uncertainty of their performance. This can be reflected by the fluctuation among different transactions. For the ease of illustration, we consider only four transactions with providers S and T, respectively, although the actual number of transactions should be much larger. These transactions are represented as $(s_1, ..., s_4)$ and $(t_1, ..., t_4)$. Table 6.1 gives these transactions with a focus on the user rating (in a scale of 1 to 5) and the latency. Finally, the aggregate QoWS values, represented as $\bar{s}$ and $\bar{t}$, obtained by averaging all transactions are given in the last row of Table 6.1.* ∎

Table 6.1 A Set of Service Transactions

	Provider S			Provider T	
TID	Rating	Latency	TID	Rating	Latency
s_1	3	25s	t_1	2	30s
s_2	2	32s	t_2	2	41s
s_3	4	23s	t_3	3	18s
s_4	2	24s	t_4	2	23s
$\bar{s}$	2.75	26s	$\bar{t}$	2.25	28s

When computing service skylines using the aggregate QoWS values, $\bar{s}$ and $\bar{t}$ can be directly used for dominance checking in Example 6.1. In this case, S dominates T. On the other hand, when the uncertainty of the QoWS is considered, we need to take a holistic view of the QoWS values from all the transactions (because the actual QoWS is captured by each of these transactions). If we take a closer look at each transaction individually, some interesting result can be discovered which is very different from using the aggregate values. For example, transaction t_3 is not dominated by any transactions of S. Since it takes a chance of $1/4$ for transaction t_3 to happen with provider T, the chance that provider S does not dominate T in practice is at least $1/4$. In fact, if all other transactions are considered, the chance that S dominates T is only $1/2$ in practice. This can be informally calculated as follows. For example, t_1 is dominated by three transactions of S (s_1, s_3, and s_4), which means it has a chance of $3/4$ to be dominated by S. Similarly, t_2 and t_4 have chances of $4/4$ and $1/4$ to be dominated by S, respectively. Considering that t_1, t_2, t_3, and t_4 all take a chance of $1/4$ to happen with provider T, the overall probability that S dominates T is $1/4 \times (3/4 + 4/4 + 0 + 1/4) = 1/2$. *This implies that the QoWS delivered by T in practice has a 50% chance that is not dominated by that delivered by S.* However, the user may believe that S is able to dominate T all the time if only the certain (i.e., the aggregate) QoWS is considered.

Incorporating the uncertainty of QoWS into service skyline analysis allows users to have a deep understanding on the real behavior of the service providers in the dynamic environment. We introduce the notion of *p-dominant service skyline* as an effective tool that facilitates service users in selecting their desired service providers with the presence of uncertainty in their QoWS. Specifically, a provider S belongs to the p-dominant service skyline if the chance that S is dominated by any other provider is less than p, where $p \in [0, 1]$, is a probability threshold. *By setting an appropriate probability threshold p, service users will gain a corresponding level of confidence (in terms of probability) that a selected provider "actually" belongs to the service skyline.* Thus, computing service skylines from uncertain QoWS provides a more meaningful and practical solution for the service optimization problem.

Computing skyline based on uncertain information poses a set of new challenges, which make it hard to adapt existing skyline approaches [14, 80, 47, 60] to computing the p-dominant skyline.

- An uncertain object is no longer a simple multi-dimensional vector. Instead, it is usually associated with some probability density function or represented by a set of instances that have the effect of approximating the probability density function when it is not available [63]. When an uncertain object is represented by a set of instances (which is usually the case for service providers), the possible large number of instances will introduce significant computational overhead for the pairwise comparison between uncertain objects.
- The dominance relationship between uncertain objects does not maintain the transitive property, which is very effective to prune the dominated data points in traditional skyline analysis. A set of uncertain object $U_1, ..., U_k$ may form a cyclic dominance relationship with probability threshold p. That is, U_1 dominates U_2 with a chance greater than p, ..., U_{k-1} dominates U_k with a chance greater than p, and U_k dominates U_1 with a chance greater than p. This is similar to the k-dominate relationship on certain objects discussed in [22]. Therefore, an uncertain object can not be pruned even if it is dominated with a chance greater than p because it may be useful for pruning other objects.

Example 6.2. Consider three providers A, B, and C. Their respective transactions record the user rating and latency. Assume, there are three A transactions: $a_1(2, 27), a_2(1, 25)$ and $a_3(2, 17)$; three B transactions: $b_1(2, 19), b_2(2, 28)$, and $b_3(3, 30)$; and two C transactions: $c_1(3, 31)$ and $c_2(3, 34)$. By setting $p = 1/3$, we have A p-dominates B and B p-dominates C but the probability that A dominates C is 0. Thus, it is not transitive. ∎

The first work, to our best knowledge, that addresses skyline analysis on uncertain data is presented by [63], in which Pei et al. presented the p-skyline and a set of efficient pruning techniques for computing the p-skyline. Uncertain data objects are represented by a set of instances in [63]. It is natural to follow this convention in computing the service skyline from uncertain QoWS because the QoWS of a service provider is usually reflected by a series of transactions. However, there are some inherent issues of applying the p-skyline to the service optimization problem. First, the p-skyline usually prefers to uncertain objects with large variances (i.e., objects that have some very good and very bad instances at the same time) [63]. However, this may contradict common users' decisions when selecting their desired providers. Furthermore, the p-skyline is very sensitive to the *noise* providers. By noise providers, we refer to the providers that deliver bad and inconsistent QoWS, which we expect to be common in the dynamic service environment. In fact, *the chance that a good and consistent provider is selected into the p-skyline will decrease exponentially with the number of noise providers.* We will come back to this with more detail in Section 6.2, where we demonstrate that the p-dominant skyline is completely robust to the number of noise providers. It is also worth noting that consistency is different from other typical quality parameters, like latency or availability because a high consistency does not necessarily implies a good quality but a low latency or a high availability does. For example, a service provider that consistently asks for a high price or response to service requests very slowly is by no means a good provider. This is also justified by the fact that the widely used QoWS models do not make consistency as one of their quality dimensions [94, 92, 46, 7].

The proposed p-dominant skyline is able to address all these issues. Computing the p-dominant service skyline provides a decent way to select the service providers that can consistently deliver good QoWS in the dynamic service environment. Since a single service provider may have a large number of transactions, checking the dominance relationship between each pair of providers is computationally expensive. Furthermore, without the transitive property, a provider that is determined not being in the p-dominant skyline cannot be pruned immediately. Thus, given a set of N providers, a brute force approach needs to check dominance against $N/2$ providers on average to determine whether a provider belongs to the p-dominant skyline or not. Efficient algorithms must be developed to compute the p-dominant skyline.

6.2 Preliminaries

We present a set of key concepts used throughout in this chapter. We then formally define the p-dominant skyline problem and further motivate the use of p-dominant skylines to tackle the service optimization problem. Table 6.2 summarizes a set of key terms.

Table 6.2 Terminologies

Term	Description
S, T	service providers
s, t	transactions with S and T
$s \succ t$	transaction s dominates transaction t
$\|S\|$	number of transactions with S
$P\{s \succ T\}$	the probability that s dominates T
$P\{S \succ T\}$	the probability that S dominates T
$P\{S\}\ (P\{s\})$	the probability that S or s in the skyline

6.2.1 Problem Definition

We start by defining the probability that provider S dominates provider T. [63] derives the dominate probability on uncertain objects from the continuous case and generalizes it to the discrete case. In contrast, we interpret this probability entirely from the discrete point of view (which suits better for the service optimization scenario). This helps provide an intuitive way to understand this probability. Similarly, we assume that a transaction with a provider is independent of transactions with other providers. We also assume that each transaction is equally like to occur with a specified provider.

Consider a service provider S whose QoWS can be presented as a set of transactions, i.e., $S = \{s_1, ..., s_{|S|}\}$. From the probability's perspective, S can be viewed as a *sample space*. The individual transactions can be regarded as a sequence of events in S that are *pairwise mutually exclusive* (i.e., only one transaction can happen at a certain point of time). Suppose that we have another service provider $T = \{t_1, ..., t_{|T|}\}$. The probability that S dominates T can be derived as follows:

$$P\{S \succ T\} = P\{(s_1 \cap (s_1 \succ T)) \cup ... \cup (s_{|S|} \cap (s_{|S|} \succ T))\}$$

$$= \sum_{i=1}^{|S|} P\{(s_i \cap (s_i \succ T))\} = \sum_{i=1}^{|S|} P\{s_i\} \times P\{s_i \succ T\}$$

Since each transaction has an equal probability to appear in S, $P\{s_i\} = \frac{1}{|S|}$. The probability that a transaction s_i dominates T given that s_i occurs is defined as the number of transactions in T that are dominated by s_i over the total number of transactions in T, i.e., $P\{s_i \succ T\} = \frac{|T_{s_i}|}{|T|}$, where $T_{s_i} = \{t | t \in T \wedge s_i \succ t\}$.

Definition 6.3. (dominate probability) The probability that S dominates T is defined as:

$$P\{S \succ T\} = \frac{1}{|S|} \times \sum_{i=1}^{|S|} \frac{|T_{s_i}|}{|T|}, \tag{6.1}$$

where $T_{s_i} = \{t | t \in T \wedge s_i \succ t\}$

■

Definition 6.4. (p-dominate) A provider S is said to p-dominate another provider T if and only if $P\{S \succ T\} \geq p$, where $0 \leq p \leq 1$, is a probability threshold. ■

Definition 6.5. (p-dominant service skyline) A provider S is in the p-dominant service skyline if and only if there does not exist any provider $T \neq S$ that p-dominates S. ■

Example 6.6. Given Eq. (6.1), we can now compute the dominate probability between service providers in Example 6.2. For instance, the probability that A dominates B can be calculated as follows:

$$P\{A \succ B\} = \frac{1}{|A|} \times \sum_{i=1}^{|A|} \frac{|B_{a_i}|}{|B|}, where \tag{6.2}$$

$$|B_{a_1}| = |\{b_j|b_j \in B \wedge a_1 \succ b_j\}| = |\{b_2\}| = 1 \tag{6.3}$$

$$|B_{a_2}| = |\{b_j|b_j \in B \wedge a_1 \succ b_j\}| = |\{\}| = 0 \tag{6.4}$$

$$|B_{a_3}| = |\{b_j|b_j \in B \wedge a_3 \succ b_j\}| = |\{b_1, b_2\}| = 2 \tag{6.5}$$

$$Thus, \ P\{A \succ B\} = \frac{1}{3} \times (\frac{1}{3} + \frac{0}{3} + \frac{2}{3}) = \frac{1}{3} \tag{6.6}$$

Similarly, we have $P\{A \succ C\} = 0$, $P\{B \succ A\} = 2/9$, $P\{B \succ C\} = 1/3$, $P\{C \succ A\} = 0$, and $P\{C \succ B\} = 0$. By setting $p = 1/3$, we have A p-dominates B and B p-dominates C. Thus, only A belongs to the 1/3-dominant service skyline. ■

Problem definition. *Given a set of service providers S and a specified probability threshold p, compute the p-dominant service skyline.* ■

6.2.2 *p-dominant Skyline Vs. p-skyline*

The notion of *p-skyline* is proposed by Pei et al. to denote the set of uncertain objects that take a probability of at least p to be in the skyline [63]. To further motivate why the p-dominant skyline is needed, we investigate the difference between the p-dominant skyline and the p-skyline in this section. We then discuss the issues of applying the p-skyline for the service optimization problem.

The probability that an uncertain object S is in the skyline is defined as follows in [63]:

$$P\{S\} = \frac{1}{|S|} \times \sum_{s \in S} P\{s\} \tag{6.7}$$

where $P\{s\}$ is the skyline probability of s and defined as:

$$P\{s\} = \prod_{T \neq S} (1 - \frac{|\{t \in T | t \succ s\}|}{|T|}) \tag{6.8}$$

Example 6.7. Given Eq. (6.7), we can now compute the skyline probability of service providers in Example 6.2. For instance, the probability that A belongs to the skyline can be calculated as follows:

$$P\{a_1\} = (1 - \frac{|\{b_1\}|}{|B|}) \times (1 - \frac{|\{\}|}{|C|}) = (1 - \frac{1}{3}) \times 1 = \frac{2}{3} \tag{6.9}$$

$$P\{a_2\} = (1 - \frac{|\{b_1\}|}{|B|}) \times (1 - \frac{|\{\}|}{|C|}) = (1 - \frac{1}{3}) \times 1 = \frac{2}{3} \tag{6.10}$$

$$P\{a_3\} = (1 - \frac{|\{\}|}{|B|}) \times (1 - \frac{|\{\}|}{|C|}) = 1 \tag{6.11}$$

$$Thus, \ P\{A\} = \frac{1}{3} \times (\frac{2}{3} + \frac{2}{3} + 1) = \frac{7}{9} \tag{6.12}$$

∎

As discovered in [63], uncertain objects with large variances (e.g., objects that have some very good and very bad instances at the same time) are usually preferred by the p-skyline. This may make it not appropriate for the service optimization problem because a consistent provider is usually more desired than the inconsistent ones.

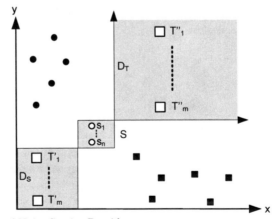

Fig. 6.1 The Effect of Noise Service Providers

In addition to the above observation, there is another hidden but maybe more serious issue of applying the p-skyline on the service optimization problem: *the chance that some good and consistent provider is selected into the skyline may be greatly reduced by other very inconsistent providers.* Given the dynamic service environment, the QoWS delivered by a certain provider could be very inconsistent. For example, it is common that a provider starts with fairly high QoWS to attract users in the very beginning and drops to a lower level later on due to various reasons (e.g., to reduce the cost). Consider a provider S that consistently delivers good QoWS. As shown in Figure 6.1, all S transactions consistently fall into the bounding rectangle in the middle. Assume that there are m providers $T_1, ..., T_m$ that deliver very inconsistent QoWS. Each of these providers has a very small subset of transactions T_i' ($|T_i'| \geq 1$) fall into the D_S area, which means that these transactions can dominate those of S. All other transactions T_i'' from each T_i fall into the D_T area, which are dominated by S. Assume w.l.o.g. that $|T_i| = |S| = n, 1 \leq i \leq m$. Thus, we have

$$P\{s\} \leq \prod_{T \neq S} (1 - \frac{1}{n}) = (1 - \frac{1}{n})^m \qquad (6.13)$$

$$P\{S\} = \frac{1}{|S|} \times \sum_{s \in S} P\{s\} \leq n(1 - \frac{1}{n})^m \qquad (6.14)$$

The above analysis shows that the probability of S is in the skyline will decrease exponentially with the increase of the number of inconsistent providers, like $T_1, ..., T_m$. For example, when $n = 0.5k$ and $m = 10k$, the probability of S is in the skyline will be below 1.01×10^{-6}. Since the size of $T_1', .., T_m'$ (i.e., good transactions) is very small, providers $T_i, ..., T_m$ can just be viewed as *noises* in the service space. Thus, computing the p-skyline is vulnerable to the side effect brought by these noises, especially when their numbers are large.

The p-dominant skyline, on the other hand, is quite robust to these noises. In particular, the increase of the number of noises will not affect the p-dominant skyline at all. Continue with the above example. $T_1, ..., T_m$ only affect the probability that S is in the p-dominant service skyline by the maximum probability that $T_1, ..., T_m$ can dominate S. We have,

$$\max(P\{T_1 \succ S\}, ..., P\{T_n \succ S\}) = \frac{|T_{\hat{i}}|}{n} \qquad (6.15)$$

$$\text{where,} \quad \hat{i} = \arg\max_i |T_i| \qquad (6.16)$$

Since for any noise provider T_i, the size of T_i' (i.e., the good transactions) should be very small (because otherwise T_i will be a good provider). Therefore, $\frac{|T_i|}{n}$ should also be very small because $T_{\hat{i}}$ is one of the noise providers. Since $\frac{|T_i|}{n}$ is independent of m, the number of noise providers (i.e., m) has no effect on the probability of S being in the p-dominant skyline. Thus, computing the p-dominant skyline ensures that providers that consistently deliver good QoWS (like S) are more likely to be included in the skyline, which is desired by the service users.

The following theorem specifies another key property of the p-dominant skyline: all providers selected by computing the (1-p)-skyline will also be included in the p-dominant service skyline. This ensures that the p-dominant skyline will not miss any really good providers, either.

Theorem 6.8. *The $(1-p)$-skyline is a subset of the p-dominant skyline, i.e., $(1-p)$-skyline $\subseteq$ p-dominant skyline.*

PROOF: Assume that there exists a provider S, such that $S \in (1-p)$-skyline and $S \notin p$-dominant skyline. Since $S \notin p$-dominant skyline, there must exist a provider T_i, such that $P\{T_i \succ S\} > p$. Thus, we have

$$P\{S \not\prec T_i\} = \frac{1}{|S|} \times \sum_{s \in S} P\{s \not\prec T_i\} < (1-p),$$

$$\text{where } P\{s \not\prec T_i\} = 1 - \frac{|\{t \in T_i | t \succ s\}|}{|T_i|}$$

On the other hand, since

$$P\{s\} = \prod_{T \neq S}(1 - \frac{|\{t \in T | t \succ s\}|}{|T|})$$

$$= P\{s \not\prec T_i\} \times \prod_{T \neq S \wedge T \neq T_i}(1 - \frac{|\{t \in T | t \succ s\}|}{|T|}),$$

we have $P\{s\} \leq P\{s \not\prec T_i\}$. Therefore,

$$P\{S\} = \frac{1}{|S|} \times \sum_{s \in S} P\{s\} \leq \frac{1}{|S|} \times \sum_{s \in S} P\{s \not\prec T_i\} < (1-p),$$

which leads to a contradiction. ∎

6.3 Computing the *p*-dominant Skyline using *p*-R-tree

We present algorithms for efficiently computing the p-dominant skyline. The algorithms are based upon a new indexing structure, called *p-R-tree*. A p-R-tree is an augmentation of the R-tree data structure to efficiently prune uncertain objects that are p-dominated by other objects. A set of heuristics are also developed in addition to the p-R-tree to efficiently find the p-dominant skyline.

6.3.1 p-R-tree

The p-R-tree is built based upon an important concept, called *p-complete dominate*. p-complete dominate offers a key property which can be used to effectively prune service providers (or uncertain objects in general).

6.3.1.1 p-Complete Dominate

Definition 6.9. (complete dominate) A transaction s is said to complete dominate another provider T if and only if $P\{s \succ T\} = 1$.   ∎

Definition 6.10. (p-complete dominate) A service provider S is said to p-complete dominate service another provider T if and only if there exists a subset of S, denoted as S', such that $\forall s \in S'$, s complete dominates T, and $\frac{|S'|}{|S|} \geq p$.   ∎

Lemma 6.11. *If S p-complete dominates T, then S p-dominates T.*
PROOF SKETCH: Based on Equation 6.1 and Definition 6.10, we have $P\{S \succ T\} = \frac{1}{|S|} \times (\sum_{s \in S'} P\{s \succ T\} + \sum_{s \in (S-S')} P\{s \succ T\}) \geq \frac{1}{|S|} \times \sum_{s \in S'} P\{s \succ T\} = \frac{1}{|S|} \times |S'| \geq p$.   ∎

Figure 6.2 (a) gives an example of the p-complete dominate relationship. A provider S is represented by its minimum bounding rectangle (MBR(S)), whose lower-left and upper-right corners are denoted by S_{min} and S_{max} respectively. The shaded area of MBR(S) (i.e., S') contains no less than $p \times |S|$ transactions. From Figure 6.2 (a) we can see for each transaction $s \in S'$, s dominates all the transactions in MBR(T). Therefore, S p-complete dominates T.

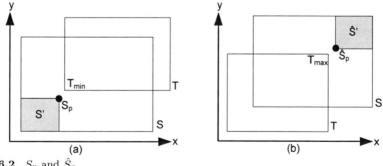

Fig. 6.2 S_p and $\hat{S}_p$

Corollary 6.12. *s complete dominates $T \Leftrightarrow s \succ T_{min}$.*
PROOF: [$\Rightarrow$] Assume that $s \not\succ T_{min}$. Thus, there must exist one dimension say d_i such that $s.d_i > T_{min}.d_i$ (assume the smaller the value is the better). Since

$T_{min} = (\min_{t \in T}\{t.d_1\}, ..., \min_{t \in T}\{t.d_{|D|}\})$, where $|D|$ is the total number of dimensions, we have $s.d_i > \min_{t \in T}\{t.d_i\}$. Assume w.l.o.g. that $t_j.d_i = \min_{t \in T}\{t.d_i\}$. Therefore, $s.d_i > t_j.d_i$. Thus, we have $s \not\succ t_j$, which contradicts that s complete dominates T.

[$\Leftarrow$] Since $s \succ T_{min}$ and $T_{min} \succeq t, \forall t \in T$, we have $s \succ t, \forall t \in T$. Hence, s complete dominates T.   ∎

Lemma 6.13. *The transitive property holds for the p-complete dominate relationship, i.e., if R p-complete dominates S, and S p-complete dominates T, then R p-complete dominates T.*

PROOF: Since R p-complete dominates S and S p-complete dominates T, there must exist $R' \subseteq R$ and $S' \subseteq S$, where $\frac{|R'|}{|R|} \geq p$ and $\frac{|S'|}{|S|} \geq p$, such that $\forall r \in R'$, r complete dominates S and $\forall s \in S'$, s complete dominates T. Due to Corollary 6.12, we have $\forall s \in S'$, $s \succ T_{min}$. Since $\forall s \in S', S_{min} \succeq s$, $S_{min} \succ T_{min}$. Also due to Corollary 6.12, we have $\forall r \in R'$, $r \succ S_{min}$. Thus, $\forall r \in R'$, $r \succ T_{min}$ and hence, R p-complete dominates T.   ∎

6.3.1.2 Building the p-R-tree

Lemma 6.13 specifies the key property behind the p-R-tree: *a provider can be pruned immediately as long as it is discovered to be p-complete dominated.* The basic steps of constructing a p-R-tree are as follows. For each S, we select a subset S' such that $|S'| \geq p \times n$, where $n = |S|$. Define $S_p = (\max_{s \in S'}\{s.d_1\}, ..., \max_{s \in S'}\{s.d_{|D|}\})$, which is the upper-right corner of $MBR(S')$. Figure 6.2 (a) gives an example of the obtained S' and S_p. Then, construct a R-tree using the S_p obtained from each S. To evaluate whether a provider S is p-complete dominated, we just issue a window query with the origin and S_{min} as the opposite corners on the p-R-tree. If the result set of the window query is not empty, S can be immediately pruned.

The only remaining issue now is how to select the subset S' from S because choosing S' inappropriately may impair the pruning power of the p-R-tree. Based on Definition 6.10 and Lemma 6.12, in order for S to p-complete dominate T, we need to have each $s \in S'$, such that $s \succ T_{min}$. We choose S' based on the following fact: $s \succ T_{min} \Rightarrow s.mindist < T_{min}.mindist$, hence $s.mindist \not< T_{min}.mindist \Rightarrow s \not\succ T_{min}$, where the *mindist* of s or T_{min} equals to the sum of its coordinates. Therefore, we should choose s that is as near to the origin as possible (to achieve a small *mindist*) to increase its chance to dominate T_{min}.

We adopt the following heuristic empowered by a binary search strategy to improve the pruning power of the p-R-tree. First, select the top $p \times n$ transactions with the smallest *mindists* from S. Then, compute $S_p^+ = (\max_{s \in S'^+}\{s.d_1\}, ..., \max_{s \in S'^+}\{s.d_{|D|}\})$, where S'^+ contains all the transactions in the MBR with S_{min} and S_p^+ as the minimum and maximum corners, respectively. Since the boundary of $MBR(S'^+)$ is formed by the maximum value of all the selected $p \times n$ transactions at each dimension, S'^{+} would typically include much more than $p \times n$ transactions. As shown in Figure 6.3 (a), the dark grey rectangle represents MBR(S'^{+}) which contains more than $p \times n$ transactions whereas the light grey rectangle contains exact $p \times n$ transactions. To make S_p close to the origin, the optimal way is to set the maximum corner of the light grey rectangle as S_p instead of directly using S_p^{+} (which is the maximum corner of S'^{+}). We use a binary search process to approach the optimal S_p. Specifically, this process takes S_p^{+} as the upper bound and searches for a MBR(S') with S_{min} as its minimum corner and contains the number of transactions within the range of $[p \times n, p \times n + \epsilon]$ (ϵ is a buffer that is set to trade precision with efficiency). The maximum corner of the obtained MBR is set to S_p.

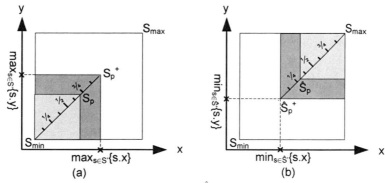

Fig. 6.3   Binary Search for Optimal S_p and $\hat{S}_p$

6.3.2 A Dual Pruning Process

Actually computing the dominate probability is a time consuming process. For providers S and T, each of which contains n transactions with a $|D|$ dimensionality, the time complexity is $n^2 \times |D|$. We present a dual pruning process which leverages the p-R-tree and a set of efficient pruning heuristics to eliminate a large portion of providers without actually computing the dominate probability.

6.3.2.1 Pruning using $\hat{S}_p$

The p-R-tree essentially leverages a subset of transactions with good performance from each provider to prune other providers. On the other hand, if a provider has a subset of transactions with bad performance, it can also be quickly pruned. Based on this observation, for each S, we select a subset $\hat{S}'$ such that $|\hat{S}'| \geq p \times n$, where $n = |S|$. Define $\hat{S}_p = (\min_{s \in \hat{S}'}\{s.d_1\}, ..., \min_{s \in \hat{S}'}\{s.d_{|D|}\})$, which is the lower-left corner of MBR($\hat{S}'$). Figure 6.2 (b) gives an example of the obtained $\hat{S}'$ and $\hat{S}_p$. If $\exists T$, such that $T_{max} \succ \hat{S}_p$, we have T_{max} complete dominates $\hat{S}'$. Hence, T p-dominates S. To improve the chance of pruning such kind of providers, we adopt a similar strategy to select $\hat{S}'$ as used to select S'. First, select top $(p \times n)$ transactions with the largest *mindists* from S to form $\hat{S}'^{+}$. Then, we use the binary search strategy as described in Sect. 6.3.1.2 to find the optimal $\hat{S}_p$ (shown in Figure 6.3 (b)). To check whether $\hat{S}_p$ is dominated by certain T_{max}, we build a R-tree (denoted as R_{max}) using the T_{max} from each provider. When S is processed, we issue a window query with the origin and $\hat{S}_p$ as the opposite corners on R_{max}. A non-empty result set implies that S is p-dominated.

The use of $\hat{S}_p$ coupled with S_p (which is used to build the p-R-tree) essentially achieves a dual pruning effect, i.e., a selected set of good transactions of S, represented by S', is used to prune other providers; on the other hand, a selected set of bad transactions of S, represented by $\hat{S}'$ is used to prune itself. Only the providers that survive this dual pruning process need to go through the dominate probability computation process, which we elaborate below.

6.3.3 Computing the Dominate Probability

If S survives the dual pruning process, we need to compute the dominate probability against other providers. In fact, the number of providers that have to go through this step is typically much less than the total number of providers (considering that they have passed the dual pruning process). We adopt a similar strategy as used in [63] (see Sect. 6.3.5 for details) to get the providers that possibly p-dominate S. We use the following approach to compute the dominate probability on S.

Consider a possible p-dominating provider, say T. Assume that the transactions in both S and T are sorted based on their *mindists*. For each $s_i \in S$ (start from the s_i with the largest *mindist*, say s_0), perform a binary search of s_i in T. Count the number of transactions in T that have a *mindist* less than that of s_i, say n_i, because only these transactions may dominate s_i. Estimate the upper bound of $\sum_i n_i$ at each step. If at certain point we know that the upper bound of $\frac{\sum_i n_i}{|T| \times |S|} < p$, stop the process and go to the next possible p-dominating provider. If we go through all the transactions and still have $\frac{\sum_i n_i}{|T| \times |S|} \geq p$, construct a R-tree using all the transactions in T that have a *mindist* less than that of s_0. We don't need to build a R-tree for each individual s_i because by doing so we have included all transactions in T that may dominate each $s_i \in S$. Then, for each s_i, issue a window query with the origin and s_i as the opposite corners to count the number of t such that $t \succ s_i$. If $\frac{\sum_i |\{t|t \succ s_i\}|}{|T| \times |S|} \geq p$, S can be pruned. If after testing all the possible p-dominating providers and S is not pruned, S is in the p-dominant skyline.

6.3.4 The Main Memory p-R-tree

To further improve the performance, our final refinement is to make the p-R-tree in memory. This is based on the observation that the p-R-tree is only used for dominance checking. When checking whether a provider S is p-complete dominated, we issue a window query on the p-R-tree (recall Sect. 6.3.1.2). As long as we can get a non-empty result set, S can be pruned. In this case, we can just compute the skyline from the disk-based p-R-tree and build a main memory p-R-tree by only using the skyline points because if S is p-complete dominated by a non-skyline point it must be p-complete dominated by at least one skyline point (which guarantees a non-empty result set). Similarly, since R_{max} is only used for dominance checking, we can also make it reside in the main memory.

Algorithm 10 Dual Pruning [Phase I]

Require: A set of service providers $\mathcal{S}$, probability threshold p
Ensure: a candidate list $\mathcal{L}$, a hash table $\mathcal{M}$
  1: **Initialization:**
  2: **for all** $S \in \mathcal{S}$ **do**
  3:     compute S_{min}, S_{max}, S_p, and $\hat{S}_p$;
  4: **end for**
  5: build R_{min}, R_{max}, and the p-R-tree;
  6: compute the skyline from the p-R-tree;
  7: build main memory R-tree, R_p and R'_{max} from the p-R-tree and R_{max}, respectively
  8: **Main procedure:**
  9: $\mathcal{L} = \phi$; $\mathcal{M} = \phi$; $\mathcal{H} = \phi$;
 10: insert the root entries of R_{min} into $\mathcal{H}$;
 11: **while** $\mathcal{H} \neq \phi$ **do**
 12:     extract the top entry e from $\mathcal{H}$;
 13:     **if** e is not dominated by R_p **then**
 14:         **if** e is an intermediate node **then**
 15:             **for all** child entry e_i of e **do**
 16:                 **if** e_i is not dominated by R_p **then**
 17:                     insert e_i into $\mathcal{H}$;
 18:                 **end if**
 19:             **end for**
 20:         **else**
 21:             insert $e.id$ into $\mathcal{M}$;
 22:             **if** $\hat{e}_p$ is not dominated by R'_{max} **then**
 23:                 insert e into $\mathcal{L}$;
 24:             **end if**
 25:         **end if**
 26:     **end if**
 27: **end while**

6.3.5 The Two Phase Algorithm

We combine different pieces into an integrated process and present a two phase algorithm in this section. The first phase leverages the p-R-tree and the pruning strategy presented in Sect. 6.3.2.1 to filter out the p-dominated providers. The remaining providers will go into the second phase, where the dominate probability will be computed on them.

As shown in Algorithm 10, phase I initializes by building R_{min} (a R-tree on S_{min}), R_{max} (a R-tree on S_{max}), and the p-R-tree. It then constructs the main memory version of the p-R-tree and R_{max}, which are denoted as R_p and R'_{max}, respectively. The main body of the algorithm performs the dual pruning process. It starts from the root node of R_{min} and inserts all its entries into the heap $\mathcal{H}$. The entry with the minimum *mindist*, say e, will be popped up. e will be first checked against with R_p (where the first level of pruning occurs). If e is dominated, then prune e. Otherwise, if e is an intermediate entry, expand it and insert all its child entries that are not dominated by R_p

into the heap. If e is a leaf (i.e., e is a provider), insert $e.id$ into the hash table $\mathcal{M}$. Then, check $\hat{e}_p$ against R'_{max} (where the second level of pruning occurs). If e is not p-dominated, insert it into the candidate list $\mathcal{L}$.

Phase II is shown in Algorithm 11. It takes as input the candidate list $\mathcal{L}$ and the hash table $\mathcal{M}$ obtained in the first phase. For each $S \in \mathcal{L}$, it computes a set $\mathcal{T}$ that possibly p-dominate S. This is done by issuing a window query with the origin and S_{max} as the opposite corners on R_{min}. For each $T \in \mathcal{T}$, it searches its id in the hash table. Only a T with an id in the hash table will be used for computing the dominate probability on S. If S is not p-dominated in the end, it is inserted into the p-dominant skyline.

Algorithm 11 Computing the Dominate Probability [Phase II]

Require: A candidate list $\mathcal{L}$, a hash table $\mathcal{M}$
Ensure: the p-dominate skyline $\mathcal{DS}$
 1: **for all** $S \in \mathcal{L}$ **do**
 2:     compute the set $\mathcal{T}$ that possibly p-dominate S;
 3:     **for all** $T \in \mathcal{T}$ **do**
 4:         search T.id in $\mathcal{M}$;
 5:         **if** T.id is in $\mathcal{M}$ **then**
 6:             compute the dominate probability of T on S;
 7:         **end if**
 8:     **end for**
 9:     **if** S is not p-dominated by all $T \in \mathcal{T}$ **then**
10:         insert S into $\mathcal{DS}$;
11:     **end if**
12: **end for**

6.3.6 Analysis

The skyline computed from the p-R-tree actually determines the region of the data space that may contain the p-dominant skyline. This region is called skyline search region (SSR) for traditional skyline analysis [60]. We name it *pSSR* (i.e., p-dominant skyline search region) in our p-dominant skyline analysis.

Lemma 6.14. *A p-dominant skyline algorithm, which leverages a R-tree R_{min} built from the S_{min} of each uncertain object S, must access each node which has a MBR that intersects the pSSR.*   ∎

Figure 6.4 shows that the entry e in R_{min} will be accessed by the algorithm although its two child nodes $S1_{min}$ and $S2_{min}$ are all dominated by the skyline computed from the p-R-tree (i.e., not in the *pSSR*).

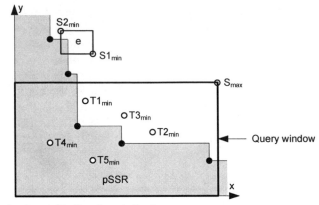

Fig. 6.4 p-dominant Skyline Search Region

6.3.6.1 Time Complexity of Phase I

The complexity of the first phase is dominated by the number of nodes in R_{min} that are accessed by the algorithm. Using the concept of *pSSR*, we can make an estimation on its upper bound. Assume that the height of R_{min} is h and there are $cand_i$ candidate nodes in the ith level of R_{min}. The total number of node accesses can be represented as

$$NA = \sum_{i=0}^{h-1} cand_i \tag{6.17}$$

To further examine how NA is related to the structure of R_{min} and the inherent characteristics of the data space, we further elaborate (6.17). Specifically, h can be specified as $1 + \lceil log_f(\frac{N}{f}) \rceil$, where N is the cardinality of the data space and f is the average fanout of a node in R_{min}. Suppose there are n_i nodes at level i and the probability that a node at level i intersects with *pSSR* is $P^i_{intsect(pSSR)}$. The candidate nodes at level i can be described as [60]

$$cand_i = n_i \times P^i_{intsect(pSSR)} \tag{6.18}$$

The number of node at level i can be specified as $n_i = \frac{N}{f^{i+1}}$. $P^i_{intsect(pSSR)}$ can be evaluated by using the node density $D_i(p)$ at level i, i.e.,

$$P^i_{intsect(pSSR)} = \int_{p \in pSSR} D_i(p)dp \tag{6.19}$$

A pessimistic upper bound for retrieving the entire skyline is given by [60] , which is $|L| \times h$. It is decided by the cardinality of the skylines (i.e., $|L|$) and the height of R_{min}. This upper bound corresponds to the situation that the algorithm needs to go through a complete path (i.e., the length of the path is h) to find each skyline point. However, multiple skyline points may be grouped into a single node or belong to the same branch of the R-tree.

In this regard, the R-tree can be viewed as a *cluster* mechanism that groups together the points with similar properties (e.g., similar coordinate values). Since the total number of node accesses is less than $|L| \times h$, we can have

$$NA = \alpha \times |L| \times h = \sum_{i=0}^{\lceil log_f(\frac{N}{f}) \rceil} \frac{N}{f^{i+1}} \times \int_{p \in pSSR} D_i(p)dp \qquad (6.20)$$

where $\alpha \in (0, 1]$ is defined as a bounding factor. From (6.17), (6.18), and (6.19), we can see that NA is determined by three factors: (1) the cardinality of the data space, (2) the fanout of the R-tree, and (3) the number of nodes that are in the *pSSR* at each level of the R-tree. Since the cardinality of the data space and the fanout of the R-tree is determined *a priori*, α is actually decided the size of the *pSSR*. A smaller *pSSR* means a smaller α, which also implies that fewer nodes need to be accessed (i.e., better performance). This justifies the heuristic strategy we use in Sect. 6.3.1.2 to improve the pruning power of the p-R-tree, which has the effect of making the upper-right corner of MBR(S') (i.e., S_p) as close to the origin as possible. Since S_p is used to build the p-R-tree and the skyline computed from the p-R-tree forms the boundary of the *pSSR*, the heuristic strategy also has the effect of making the boundary as close to the origin as possible, which, at the same time, makes the *pSSR* as small as possible.

6.3.6.2 Time Complexity of Phase II

The time complexity of the second phase is dominated by the cost for computing the dominate probability on each provider in the candidate list.

Lemma 6.15. *If provider S is pruned by the p-R-tree, it is guaranteed not to be used for computing the dominate probability against any other provider T.*
PROOF SKETCH: In Phase I of the algorithm, only the providers whose MBRs have a lower-left corner fall into the *pSSR* (i.e., not dominated by the p-R-tree) are inserted into the hash table $\mathcal{M}$. Phase II of the algorithm searches each possible dominating provider in $\mathcal{M}$ before using it to compute the dominate probability. This guarantees that any provider S pruned by the p-R-tree is not used for computing the dominate probability. ∎

Figure 6.4 shows the results returned from a window query with the origin and S_{max} as the opposite corners on R_{min}. There are five providers returned including $T1, ..., T5$, among which only $T4_{min}$ and $T5_{min}$ fall into the *pSSR*. Since $T1_{min}$, $T2_{min}$, and $T3_{min}$ are outside the *pSSR* (which means $T1, T2$, and $T3$ are pruned by the p-R-tree), they are not used for computing the dominate probability due to Lemma 6.15.

Assume that for each provider $S \in \mathcal{L}$, a set $\mathcal{T}_S$ of possible dominating providers are returned from the window query. Also assume that a set $\mathcal{T}_S^p \subset$

$\mathcal{T}_S$ is pruned by the p-R-tree. Suppose that the average cost for actually computing the dominate probability on a pair of providers is $\mathcal{C}$. Thus, the total time complexity of Phase II is

$$\sum_{s\in\mathcal{L}} |\mathcal{T}_S - \mathcal{T}_S^p| \times \mathcal{C} \qquad (6.21)$$

Equation 6.21 does not count the cost for searching the hash table for each provider in $\mathcal{T}_S$, which can be neglected when compared with the average cost for computing the dominate probability on a pair of providers.

6.4 Experimental Study

We report our experimental results in this section. We run our experiments on a PC with AMD Athlon 64*2 Dual Core 2.0GHz CPU and 1 GB of RAM. The algorithms are implemented in Java. The uncertain QoWS data of service providers are generated by following the approach described in [63]. In particular, the center of a provider's QoWS is generated with each of the following three distributions: independent, anti-correlated, and correlated [14]. Based on the center, a bounding box is generated which contains all the transactions with this provider. A certain number of transactions with an upper bound t are uniformly distributed in this bounding box. A total number n of such providers are thus generated, each of which has d QoWS attributes. We leverage R*-trees to implement the proposed p-R-tree. Table 6.3 lists these parameters and their default values.

Table 6.3 Parameters and Key Terms

Parameter	Description	Default
d	Dimensionality of the QoWS	4
n	Cardinality of the providers	$10k$
p	Probability threshold	0.3
t	Maximum transactions per provider	400
R_p	Skyline on S_p	N/A
R_{max}	Skyline on S_{max}	N/A
$PdSky$	p-dominant skyline	N/A
TP	Two-phase algorithm	N/A
BA	Baseline algorithm	N/A

6.4.1 Size of the p-dominant skylines

We study the size of the p-dominant skylines (denoted as *PdSky*) w.r.t. d, p, and n in this section. We also compute the skylines on S_p and S_{max} (denoted as R_p and R_{max}, respectively) to compare how the sizes of the p-dominant skylines vary from that of the traditional skylines.

Figure 6.5 shows that the size of *PdSky* follows a similar trends as traditional skylines with the increase of dimensionality. With p set to 0.3, the sizes of *Pdsky* are also similar to those of R_p and R_{max} (except for the correlated case, although the sizes can still be regarded as in the same scale). The sizes of the three skylines exhibit very different behaviors w.r.t. p, as shown in Figure 6.6. As expected, the probability threshold p has a significant effect on the size of the *PdSky*, which keeps increasing as p increases. The size of R_{max} is insensitive to p at all because S_{max} does not change with p. The size of R_p varies very slightly with p. This is in that although S_p may change with p, the size of R_p should still stay rather stable because d, n, and the data distribution (the distribution of S_p roughly follows the same distribution as the center of S) are fixed. In contrast to d and p, n has no obvious effect on the sizes of the skylines as shown in Figure 6.7. We vary n from 2k to 10k and find that the sizes of the three skylines not strictly keep increasing as n increases but they share the same trends, i.e., they increase and decrease simultaneously.

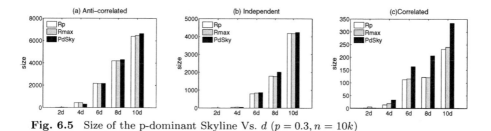

Fig. 6.5   Size of the p-dominant Skyline Vs. d ($p = 0.3, n = 10k$)

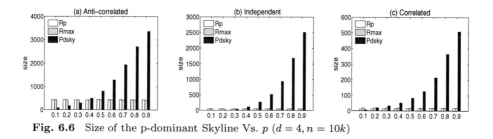

Fig. 6.6   Size of the p-dominant Skyline Vs. p ($d = 4, n = 10k$)

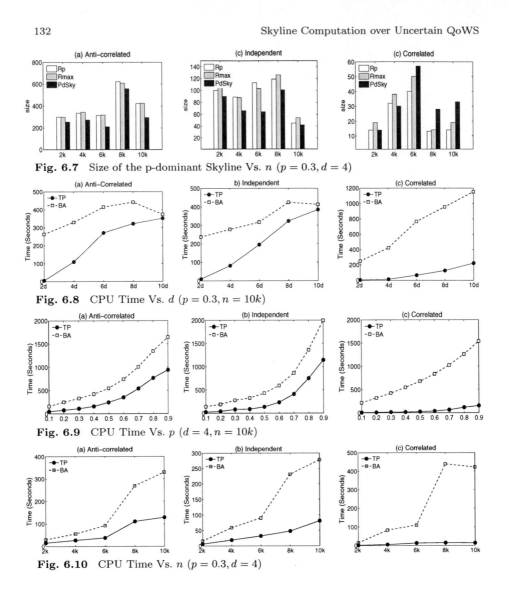

Fig. 6.7   Size of the p-dominant Skyline Vs. n $(p = 0.3, d = 4)$

Fig. 6.8   CPU Time Vs. d $(p = 0.3, n = 10k)$

Fig. 6.9   CPU Time Vs. p $(d = 4, n = 10k)$

Fig. 6.10   CPU Time Vs. n $(p = 0.3, d = 4)$

6.4.2 Performance and Scalability

We study the performance of the proposed two-phase algorithm with Figures 6.8 to 6.10. We develop a baseline algorithm (referred to as *BA*) for comparison purpose. *BA* is implemented without the dual-pruning process. It mainly relies on the technique presented in Sect. 6.3.3, i.e., for each provider, it first identifies the possible dominating providers and then computes the dominating probability against each of them.

Figure 6.8 shows that *TP* is consistently more efficient than *BA* by varying d from 2 to 10. For anti-correlated and independent QoWS (shown in Figures 6.8 (a) and (b)), the performance difference between *TP* and *BA* decreases with d. This is because that the size of *PdSky* increases significantly with d and the number of providers pruned by the dual pruning process decreases accordingly. In addition, as d increases, the data space becomes sparser, which reduces the number of possible dominating providers. This explains why *BA* performs more efficiently on a 10d space than an 8d space with anti-correlated and independent QoWS. For correlated QoWS, on the other hand, the size of the *PdSky* remains to be relatively small even for a large dimensionality. Therefore, the dual pruning process still removes a large portion of providers (see next section for details). Moreover, since the correlated QoWS are located closely to the line from $(0,...,0)$ to $(1,...,1)$, the possible dominating providers resulted from the window query may remain to be large even for large dimensions. This makes the running time of *BA* keep increasing with d. These aggregate effects make the performance difference between *TP* and *BA* increases with d (as shown in Figure 6.8 (c)). Figure 6.9 and 6.10 compare *TP* and *BA* w.r.t. p and n. *TP* is faster than BA in a consistent manner and its performance advantage over *BA* becomes more obvious with both increasing p and n.

6.4.3 Pruning Efficiency

Figures 6.11 to 6.13 demonstrate the pruning capacity by the different phases of the *TP* algorithm. Since Phase I of the algorithm uses a dual pruning strategy, we further separate the providers that are pruned by the p-R-tree (i.e., by comparing S_{min} with R_p) and those pruned by R_{max} (i.e, by comparing $\hat{S}_p$ with R_{max}).

As shown in Figures 6.11 (a) and (b), the overall pruning efficiency of the dual pruning process is fairly significant for relatively low-dimensional spaces (e.g., $d \leq 4$) on anti-correlated and independent QoWS. As d increases, the dual pruning efficiency decrease accordingly. This is due to the increase on the size of the p-dominant skyline, which can also can be reflected by the total pruning percentage by both of the two phases in *TP*. For correlated QoWS, the dual pruning efficiency remains significant even for high-dimensional spaces (as shown in Figures 6.11 (c)). Figure 6.12 shows the dual pruning efficiency w.r.t. p. The pruning power only drops very slightly when p increases. Figure 6.13 indicates that the pruning efficiency is not very sensitive to n. Another important observation is that the pruning power of the dual pruning process mainly comes from the p-R-tree for the three types of QoWS distributions. This is because that we apply the p-R-tree first in *TP* so that a large portion of providers that can also be pruned by checking $\hat{S}_p$ will be taken away by the p-R-tree.

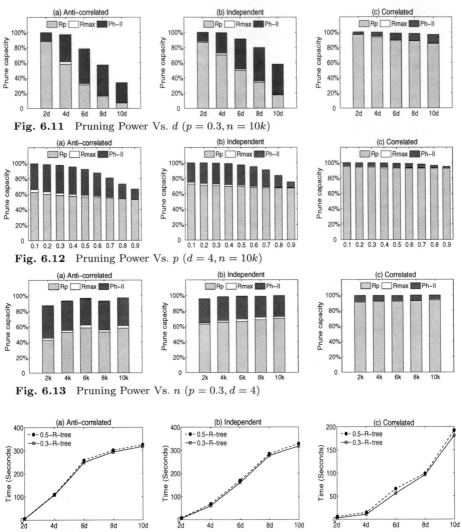

Fig. 6.11   Pruning Power Vs. d ($p = 0.3, n = 10k$)

Fig. 6.12   Pruning Power Vs. p ($d = 4, n = 10k$)

Fig. 6.13   Pruning Power Vs. n ($p = 0.3, d = 4$)

Fig. 6.14   0.5-R-tree Vs. 0.3-R-tree

6.4.4 Computing p-dominant Skyline with $(p + \delta)$-R-tree

Since the probability threshold p can be specified at large in a service query, it is not feasible to construct a p-R-tree *a priori* for each possible p. We observe that if a provider can be pruned by a p'-R-tree ($p' \geq p$), it will not appear in the p-dominant skyline. Therefore, for an arbitrary probability threshold p, we can always use a pre-constructed $(p+\delta)$-R-tree to compute the p-dominant skyline. In this section, we compare the performance of computing the 0.3-

dominant skyline with a 0.3-R-tree and a 0.5-R-tree (i.e., $\delta = 0.2$) w.r.t. d. As shown in Figure 6.14, the $(p + 0.2)$-R-tree can efficiently compute the p-dominant skyline and the performance difference with the actual p-R-tree is very small.

Chapter 7
Related Work

The proliferation of Web services is fostering a very active research area [82, 52, 54, 53, 10, 20, 91, 29, 18]. We give an overview of some work in this area which are most closely related to our work. Since the field of Web service research is still in its infancy, there is little foundational work to date.

7.1 Web Service Querying and Optimization

In [76], a Web Service Management System (WSMS) is proposed to enable optimized querying of Web services. A Web service $WS_i(\mathcal{X}_i^b, \mathcal{Y}_i^f)$ is modeled as a virtual table in the proposed WSMS. The values of attributes in $\mathcal{X}_i$ must be specified whereas the values of attributes in $\mathcal{Y}_i$ are retrieved. An algorithm is proposed to optimized access Web services. The optimization algorithm takes as input the classical Select-Project-Join queries over Web services. It arranges Web services in a query based on a cost model and returns an pipelined execution plan with minimum total running time of the query. In our service query optimization framework, we adopt a formal service model. The service model goes beyond the simple function call by effectively capturing the key features of Web services: functionality, behavior, and quality. The service calculus is proposed based on the service model. It enables users to declaratively query Web services based on these features. The optimization algorithm in [76] only considers the total running time. In contrast, we adopt a two-phase optimization process. Both the response time and the quality of Web service are optimized.

In [32], a search engine, called Woogle, is proposed to support Web service query. In contrast to the simple keyword-based query, Woogle goes a step further by providing a more flexible and precise Web service search. It adopts machine learning mechanisms to determine the similarity between the desirable operations and targeted operations. Woogle takes an information re-

Q. Yu and A. Bouguettaya, *Foundations for Efficient Web Service Selection*, DOI 10.1007/978-1-4419-0314-3_7, © Springer Science+Business Media, LLC 2009

trieval approach to measure the similarity between Web service descriptions, including the input and output of services.

In [59], a query model is proposed that offers complex and optimized query functionalities for Web services. The query model consists of three levels: query level, virtual level, and concrete level. The query level is composed of a set of relations that facilitate formulating and submitting declarative queries. The virtual level contains a set of virtual operations which represent the space of Web services within a given application domain in a generic way. The concrete level denotes the space of Web services offered on the Web. The query model uses the predefined mapping rules to capture the relationship between relations and virtual operations. Specifically, the mapping rule can represent relations at the query level using virtual operations at the virtual level. The designer can thus provide a specific view of the application domain by defining a mapping rule that represents a relation using a set of virtual operations from that domain. Users can directly use relations as queries to access Web services. Our approach goes beyond this *ad hoc* query model by proposing a solid foundation, upon which algorithms can be developed for optimizing service queries.

In [95], a composite service optimization approach is proposed based on several quality of service parameters. Composite services are represented as a state-chart. The optimization problem is tackled by finding the best Web services to execute a composite service in the form of a linear programming problem. Our work focuses on Web service query instead of generating composite services. We adopt a two-phase optimization strategy. In the first phase, the query optimizer transforms an algebraic expression into the most efficient one. It then performs the QoWS optimization in the second phase to select the service execution plan with the best quality.

In [51], a QoS ontology has been defined for Web services. However, this work does not seem to formulate how to measure the QoS parameters clearly. Additionally, it does not specify how to aggregate all these parameters for service evaluation.

7.2 Evaluation of Web Service Deployment Systems

We present a representative set of WS deployment systems in this section. These systems adopt different technologies to provide the functionalities identified by the WSMS framework. These include interoperation, security/privacy, QoWS, and management. The evaluation only covers the most representative systems for the sake of space.

There are some other standardization effort underway to full support for semantic Web services. For example, the Semantic Web Services Initiative Architecture (SWSA) committee focuses on providing architecture support for deploying semantic Web services [16]. It has identified a set of requirements for building a semantic Web service architecture. The architecture supports a three-phase interaction with semantic Web services: discovery, engagement, and enactment. Architectural requirements are identified for each interaction phase. Instead of building concrete software components, SWSA aims to generalize the protocols and functional descriptions of capacities across a variety of semantic Web service architectures. This enables specific components that are consistent with the proposed general model to interoperate with one another.

7.2.1 Research Prototypes

In this section, we present a set of WS deployment systems: CMI, Meteor, SELF-SERV, WebDG, AgFlow, WSXM, and IRS.

CMI

CMI (*Collaboration Management Infrastructure*) [6, 36] provides architectural support to manage collaboration processes. The kernel component of CMM is a *Core Model* (CORE). CORE provides a common set of primitives shared by all of its extensions. These primitives fall into two categories – *activity states* and *resources*. Activity states can be either *generic* or *application-specific*. Generic activity states follow the convention of the Workflow Management Coalition [89]. They capture activity behaviors that are independent of applications. Application-specific activity states enable the precise modeling of the peculiar applications. CORE identifies several primary resource types for the activity execution. For example, data resources refer to the workflow internal data. Helper resources refer to auxiliary programs that help implement the basic activities.

The CORE extensions include the *Coordination Model* (CM), the *Service Model* (SM), and the *Awareness Model* (AM). CM coordinates participants and automates process enactment. CM provides two types of advanced primitives: *activity placeholders* and *repeated optional dependencies*. Activity placeholders enable the run-time service selection. They represent services in a process as activity types at specification time. At run time, a concrete activity replaces the activity placeholder to construct an executable process. A resolution policy helps ensure the syntactic and semantic compatibility when replacing the placeholder by an actual activity. Repeated optional dependencies specify the invocation place of a activity in a control flow path of a process. They also specify the number of invocations of the given activity to accomplish the application's objective. The SM provides rich semantics to describe services. It introduces the notion of service ontologies to capture the semantics of services. In addition, the SM uses Quality of Service (QoS) as an important non-functional parameter to characterize services and their providers. The resolution policy can choose the service with the best QoS to optimize the execution of a process. The Awareness Model monitors the process related events. It allows authorized composition and delivery of such events only to closely related process participants.

METEOR

METEOR [19] is a workflow management platform that supports QoS management and service composition. It sets up a QoS model to describe the nonfunctional issues of the workflow. The QoS model consists of four parameters, including time, cost, reliability, and fidelity. For each parameter, the description of the operational runtime behavior of a task is composed of two classes of information: basic and distributional. The basic class specifies the minimum value, average value, and maximum value the parameter can take in a given task. The distributional class specifies a constant or of a distribution function (such as Exponential, Normal, and Uniform) which statistically describes a task's behavior at runtime. The values in the basic class are used by mathematical methods to calculate workflow QoS metrics. The distributional class information is used by simulation systems to compute workflow QoS. METEOR forms a mathematical model that collectively uses all QoS parameters. The mathematical model computes the overall QoS of workflow. It can serve as a guide to predict, estimate, and analyze the QoS of production of workflow.

METEOR extends DAML-S to describe Web services. The enriched service description includes three parts of information: syntactic description, semantic description, and operational metrics, such as QoS parameters. All of this information helps match the service object with a corresponding service template. METEOR also provides registry services to enable the advertisement and discovery of Web services. The workflow management system executes the composite services and also handles runtime exceptions using a case-based reasoning mechanism.

SELF-SERV

SELF-SERV is a platform for Web services composition [11]. It aims to provide a declarative mechanism to compose Web services. It defines a peer-to-peer mode to support scalable execution of composite Web services. SELF-SERV uses a *state chart* to model the flow of component service operations. It integrates *service containers* into its service composition platform. A service container consists of a set of Web services with common functionalities. The container determines which service is selected to execute. It carries out the selection dynamically and puts off the selection until the invocation time. The service selection is based on a set of QoWS metrics and their relative weights. The service container also handles change management. It provides operations to monitor services, notify the changes, and make reactions to the changes. SELF-SERF relies on a set of state coordinators to enable the scalable execution of composite services. It generates a state coordinator for each state in the state chart. The state coordinator determines when to enter its associated state depending on the notification of other coordinators. Once a state has been entered, the coordinator invokes the services and retrieves the results. The coordinator then notifies other coordinators when it completes the execution of the service. Routing tables maintain the information required by a coordinator. The information may include preconditions for entering a state and post actions that notify successive coordinators.

WebDG

Digital government has turned to be a major application area of Web services. WebDG is proposed based on the available Web service technologies [56]. It aims to provide high quality e-government services by improving the interacting mechanism between government and citizens. Two major contributions make WebDG distinguish itself from other e-government service suppliers. The first one is that it introduces the privacy-preserving scheme into Web services. This is among the leading efforts to combine privacy protection with Web services. While the second contribution is that it realizes the automatic service composition based on the semantic feature of Web services.

WebDG enforces privacy from the technology point of view but not merely depends on the trust of involved entities. It constructs a three-layered privacy model, including *user privacy*, *service privacy*, and *data privacy*. Each layer defines its own privacy policy respectively. Obeying these privacy policies, WebDG implements two privacy preserving schemes, including *DFilter* and *PPM*. These two schemes guarantee that necessary credentials are the keys to access the requested operation. Service composition is a necessity for most Web service systems because a single service could hardly fulfill all requirements from a user. WebDG achieves its automatic service composition resorting to the ontology notion. According to the semantic features of the services, WebDG defines two ontologies for service operations, namely, *Category* and *Type*. The semantic composability rule is derived based on these ontologies. It states that two operations can be composed with each other semantically if their Categories and Types are compatible respectively. WebDG also implements a composition template to evaluate the soundness of the service composition .

AgFlow

AgFlow is a QoS-aware middleware for Web service composition [95]. It uses ontologies to model the component services. The data types follow the XML specification and the message exchange relies on the data flow approach. The orchestration model is specified using statecharts and generated by the programming-based composition scheme. AgFlow defines a QoS model to evaluate Web services from five quality aspects: price, duration, reputation, success execution rate, and availability. Users can specify their preferences by assigning weights to each of these quality parameters. AgFlow proposes two planning strategies, local and global, to select the proper component services. The candidate composition plans are evaluated against an objective function, whereby the optimal plan with the highest objective value can be selected. Users' constraints are also considered during the planning. The global strategy can adapt to the dynamic changes in the service environment. When some component service becomes unavailable or significant changes occurs to its QoS, a re-planning process will be triggered. The re-planning is to enable the composite service to remain optimal in a dynamic environment. The performance of AgFlow is efficient when there is a small number of tasks to be accomplished by the composition. However, as the number of tasks increases, the response time of AgFlow exhibits an exponential growth. This situation becomes even more severe when re-planning is required by the composition.

WSMX and IRS-III

Web Service Modeling eXecution environment (WSMX) [86] is the reference implementation of WSMO. It provides an event-based service oriented framework for dynamic service discovery, selection, mediation, and invocation. The core of WSMX architecture is the WSMX manager. It has several major components, including *resource manager*, *discovery*, *selector*, and *mediator*. The resource manager is used to manage the repositories that store WSMO entities and other system-specific information. WSMO entities include Web services, goals, ontologies, and mediators. The WSMX discovery provides a three-step solution for service location. First, *goal discovery* is to map a user request to a predefined, formalized goal in the goal repository. Second, *Web service discovery* is to map the formalized goal to the formalized service description in the service repository. During this process, a Web service with the capability that matches the goal would be returned. Finally, *service discovery* is to map the formalized service description to the concrete service. The WSMX selector helps choose the "best" Web service returned from a set of matching Web services. Various selection criteria as well as users' preference can be applied to select the optimal Web service. The WSMX mediator is used to mediate heterogeneous entities. WSMX provides two kinds of mediators: *data mediators* and *Process mediator*. Data mediators are used to address semantic dissimilarity between data from different sources. Process mediators provide a runtime analysis and adjustment of mismatching between communication patterns from service requesters and providers. The WSMX manager controls operational flow to react to incoming requests. WSMX provides an interface to accept user requests. Once a service request is submitted, the WSMX discovery and WSMX selector locate the services that match the request and return the optimal one on demand. IRS-III (Internet Reasoning Service) is another reference implementation of WSMO [31]. It is a framework for description, location, composition of Web services. IRS-III provides two methods for creating semantic Web services, including browser-based and Java API. The IRS-III ontology adopts and extends WSMO. The additional attributes include a new type of mediator, gw-mediator. The gw-mediator is used for service discovery. An applicability function is used for selecting Web services.

7.2.2 Discussion of Web Service Deployment Platforms

In this section, we evaluate and compare different Web service deployment systems using the proposed WSMS. We first conduct the evaluation by mapping these systems onto the WS interoperation framework. This helps reflect how each system achieves the WS interoperability. We examine the different layers in the interoperation framework, including communication, messaging, representation, discovery, and processes. We then evaluate the deployment systems based on other key components in the WSMS: security/privacy, management, and QoWS. This helps reflect the functionalities of each system for dealing with other issues of WS deployment in addition to WS interoperability.

Table 7.1 WS Deployment Systems vs layers in the Interoperation Framework

Systems	Communication	Messaging	Representation
METEOR	Java RMI	Not specified	DAML-S, QoS model
CMI	HTTP, CORBA	Not specified	Service model, ontologies
SELF-SERV	HTTP	SOAP	WSDL
WebDG	HTTP	SOAP	WSDL, ontologies
AgFlow	HTTP	SOAP	WSDL, ontologies
WSMX	Not specified	SOAP	WSMO, WSML
IRS-III	HTTP	SOAP	WSMO, IRS-III ontology

Table 7.2 WS Deployment Systems vs layers in the Interoperation Framework (Cont'd)

Systems	Discovery	Processes
METEOR	registry service	Workflow engine
CMI	Service broker, advertisement	State machine-based model
SELF-SERV	UDDI	State charts
WebDG	UDDI	Composition rules, QoC Model, and composition template
AgFlow	UDDI	Statecharts
WSMX	Ontology repository, WSMX repository	Event manager
IRS-III	PSM	Task specification

Tables 7.1 and 7.2 compare the representative Web service deployment systems using layers in the WS interoperation framework. For instance, WebDG uses HTTP at the communication layer. It depends on the three key Web service standards—SOAP, WSDL, and UDDI—for messaging, representation, and discovery. In addition, WebDG also uses ontologies to describe the semantic features of Web services. At the WS processes layer, WebDG provides a set of mechanisms to compose Web services automatically. It uses the composition rules to check the semantic and syntactic composability of Web services. The composition plan is optimized based on the QoC (Quality of Composition) model. A composition template is used to evaluate the soundness of the composition.

Table 7.3 Deployment systems vs key components in the WSMS

Systems	Security	Privacy	QoWS
METEOR	Not specified	Not specified	Time, cost, reliability, and fidelity
CMI	Role-based access control	Not specified	Services attached with a set of QoS attributes
SELF-SERV	Not specified	Not specified	Weighted QoWS parameters
WebDG	Not specified	Three-layered privacy model	Not specified
AgFlow	Not specified	Not specified	Price, duration, reputation, success execution rate, and availability
WSMX	Not specified	Not specified	Accuracy, cost, network-related time, reliability, robustness, scalability, security, trust
IRS-III	Not specified	Not specified	Accuracy, cost, network-related time, reliability, robustness, scalability, security, trust

Tables 7.3 and 7.4 compare the same set of systems using the other key components in the proposed WSMS. For instance, RosettaNet adopts digital certification and digital signatures to ensure security to interact with Web services. The PIP of RosettaNet contains a transaction layer to provide

Table 7.4 Deployment systems vs key components in the WSMS (Cont'd)

System	Transaction	Change Management	Optimization	Monitoring
METEOR	Not specified	Not specified	Mathematical model to compute the overall QoS of workflow	Not specified
CMI	Coordination model	Scoped roles	Resolution policy for QoS based service selection	Awareness Model
SELF-SERV	Not specified	Service containers for monitoring changes	Not specified	Service containers for notifying changes and make reactions
WebDG	Not specified	Not specified	Quality of Composition model	Not specified
AgFlow	Not specified	Re-planning	Integer programming	Not specified
WSMX	Not specified	Not specified	WSMX selector	Not specified
IRS-III	Not specified	Not specified	Applicability function	Not specified

transaction support for the business processes. Privacy, change management, optimization, monitoring, and QoWS are not specified in RosettaNet.

Chapter 8
Conclusions

The development of Web services has so far mostly been the result of standardization bodies usually operating on a consensus basis and driven by market considerations. In this context, innovation and long-term market effects are not usually primary concerns. Because of the global nature of the Web, the standardization process has so far been very fragmented, leading to competing and potentially incompatible Web service infrastructures. Many companies have invested very heavily in Web services technologies (Microsoft's .NET, IBM's Websphere, SUN's J2EE, to name a few). These efforts have resulted in a fast-growing number of Web services being made available. The envisioned business model is expected to include a whole community of Web service providers that will compete to provide Web services. It is important that this investment produce the expected results. To maximize the benefits of this new technology, there is a need to provide a sound and clean methodology for specifying, selecting, optimizing, and composing Web services. This needs to take place within a secure environment. The underlying foundation will enable designers and developers to reason about Web services to produce efficient Web Service Management Systems.

8.1 Summary

In this book, for the first time, we describe a complete and comprehensive architecture for a Web Service Management System (WSMS). The presented WSMS are expected to provide a systematic support to organize, manipulate, and access Web services as first class objects. We also take an initiative step for building such a WSMS. We propose a foundational framework for service query optimization that will serve as a key building block for the expected WSMS. We summarize the major content of this book as follows.

Foundational Service Framework – Current Web service technologies are mainly standard-based. The successful experience from the history of

Q. Yu and A. Bouguettaya, *Foundations for Efficient Web Service Selection*,
DOI 10.1007/978-1-4419-0314-3_8, © Springer Science+Business Media, LLC 2009

databases demonstrated the importance of having a theoretical underpinning. The field of databases only enjoyed widespread acceptance after the relational model was proposed. The relational model set up the theoretical foundation for database research. The first step of our research was thereby to define a foundation for Web service research. The proposed service foundation centers around a formal service model. The service model relies on graph theories to capture a set of key features of Web services within an application domain. The service calculus and algebra are defined based on the service model. The physical implementation of the algebraic operators enables the generation of SEPs that can be directly used by users to access services. Two optimization algorithms are proposed based on a score function to efficiently process a service query and select the SEP with the best user desired QoWS.

Multi-objective Service Query Optimization – The proposed query optimization algorithms rely on a score function to select SEPs. The issue is that they require users to specify their preference on different quality parameters as numeric weights. This is a demanding task and the users may miss their desired providers if they cannot precisely specify the weights. The multi-objective optimization completely removes user intervention from service selection. We use service skylines to enable the multi-objective service query optimization. The ability to index the inherent dynamic SEP space also comes as a result of the use of operation (set) graphs in the service model. Analytical and experimental results show that the proposed indexing scheme is quite effective and efficient.

Computing Service Skylines over Sets of Services – As the number of services increases, the possible combinations between them also increase rapidly. This results in a large SEP space. Therefore, efficiently skyline computation algorithms are required that can scale to a large number of services. We developed three algorithms that include a baseline one pass algorithm, OPA, a dual progressive algorithm, DPA, and a bottom up algorithm, BUA. DPA employs an expansion tree and a parent table to achieve progressiveness and pipelineability. BUA further improves DPA with good scalability and orders of magnitude of efficiency through a powerful early pruning strategy. We experimentally evaluated the algorithms and demonstrated that BUA is an efficient and scalable algorithm in computing multi-service skylines.

Skyline Computation over Uncertain QoWS – The dynamic service environment determines that the advertised QoWS may not reflect the actual performance of service providers. Therefore, the QoWS is inherently uncertain. We introduce a new concept, called p-dominant skyline, to address the uncertainty of QoWS. We present a p-R-tree indexing structure and a dual pruning process to efficiently compute the p-dominant skyline. Our experimental results demonstrate the effectiveness of the proposed algorithm.

8.2 Directions for Future Research

We identify the important directions for future research: ontology management for Web services, QoWS management, service model extension, reversed two-phase service query optimization, subspace service skyline computation, and uncertain QoWS stream processing.

8.2.1 Ontology Management for Web Services

Ontologies empower Web services with rich semantics. They help enrich the service description and ease the service advertisement and discovery process. Ontologies offer an effective organization mechanism to deal with the large number, dynamics, and heterogeneity of Web services. Service ontologies are essentially organized in a distributed manner to adapt to the large scale of the Web. Service ontologies are formed based on Web services' domains of interest. Typically, a service ontology contains a set of standard terms to describe service classes. It also contains some inference rules to express complex relations between service classes. As the service model presented in Chapter 3 offers a uniformed view of various services within the same application domain, a potential issue is the mapping between different service ontologies. Cross-ontology interactions between Web services may bring terms and rules from one ontology to another. Interpreting and reasoning information from other ontologies precisely and efficiently is crucial for cross-ontology service integrations. Existing efforts in data integration mainly rely on a centralized mediation mechanism [34]. However, the centralized approach can hardly fit into the large scale of service ontologies on the Web. Since ontologies have become a key component for Web service description and organization, an effective mechanism to realize mappings of different ontologies would become increasingly important.

8.2.2 QoWS Management

The current optimization approach relies on the knowledge of the quality information from the service instances. A key extension is to develop quality management mechanisms that can monitor the performance of service providers and precisely report their quality values. The reputation-based approaches can also be used to evaluate the trustworthiness of service providers in reporting their QoWS. In addition, it would also be interesting to consider the missing quality values that may be common in real-world scenarios. Work on fuzzy-set based querying (e.g., SQL-F [15]) may be relevant for handling the situation of missing values.

8.2.3 Service Model Extension

The current service model assumes an "And" relationship between multiple dependency constraints in a service graph. An interesting direction is to integrate the "Or" semantic into the service model in future research. By incorporating the "Or" semantic, there might be multiple service execution paths and each execution path can be instantiated into a set of SEPs. This makes the optimization process more complicated. There are two promising approaches to deal with it: 1) include path expressions into the service queries, which enables users to specify their desired operation(set) graphs so that only one service execution path will be generated; 2) extend the current optimization approach to enable the selection of the operation(set) graphs and their corresponding SEPs.

8.2.4 Reversed Two-phase Service Query Optimization

We presented a two-phase service query optimization algorithm in Chapter 3. In the first phase, we find an efficient service query plan (referred to as SQP) and execute this SQP to generate a set of candidate SEPs. In the second phase, we find the SEP with the best QoWS. The two-phase algorithm essentially performs functional optimization in its first phase to locate all functionally feasible SEPs. It then performs non-functional optimization to select the SEP with the best quality. An interesting direction to explore is performing non-functional optimization before functional optimization in the service query optimization process. This will have the effect of filtering out service instances with bad QoWS before actually querying their functionalities. Therefore, there will be no need to generate SEPs from these service instances at all, which could reduce both the processing time and the space that is used to store these SEPs. A promising solution is to leverage the service skyline computation techniques for non-functional optimization. Then, functional optimization will only need to be performed on the skyline service instances, because other instances are dominated on all user interested quality aspects.

8.2.5 Subspace Service Skyline

Both OGI and BBS4SEP are based on a R-tree index, which are optimized for a fixed set of dimensions (and operations in the context of service skyline). It would be interesting to extend these approaches to efficiently compute service skylines on varying number of QoWS attributes. One possible approach is to build an index an all attributes. However, this has an issue of so called "curse of dimensionality" [13]. A suitable solution for the service skyline problem is to identify the typical usage patterns of service users. This is practical for specific service domains because the user interested operations and QoWS attributes usually converges to a small number of candidates. A more general solution may be to extend the Skyline Cube approach [93, 64, 81] and adapt it to the service skyline problem.

8.2.6 Uncertain QoWS Stream Processing

In our p-dominant service skyline model, each service provider is represented as a set of static transactions. A promising future direction is to model these transactions in a streaming manner, which is highly time sensitive. In another word, each transaction occurs at a certain time (or with a certain timestamp). Users typically take more interest in the more recent transactions that more precisely reflect the recent behavior of the corresponding service provider. It is interesting to integrate the sliding window model to our p-dominant skyline computation framework. This allows users to get the query result for the current sliding window [45].

8.2.7 Failure Recovery in Service Query Optimization

Service query optimization targets at the service providers that can offer the best QoWS. However, a viable and robust Web service solution also needs to have the capacity to deal with failures because the selected SEP may fail to execute due to various reasons. Failure recovery is a crucial issue for proper and effective delivery of Web service functionalities. In traditional database and distributed computing systems, failures are treated as *exceptions*. Since failures rarely happen in such fixed and well-controlled environment, some expensive mechanisms are often adopted for recovery from failures. For instance, transactions with ACID properties are the major tools to deal with failures in traditional database systems. Mobile computing is another major application area for failure recovery techniques [50, 57, 66]. In a mobile environment, failures are more prone to happen due to multiple reasons, such as physical damage, lost of mobile hosts, power limitation, and connectivity problems. The mobile computing community would treat failures as *rules* rather than exceptions due to their high occurrence probability. Checkpoint-based recovery is a representative technique used in mobile environment. Web services are autonomous and loosely coupled. They interact dynamically without *a-priori* knowledge of each other. Therefore, failures in Web service environment are expected to happen frequently. Design of an effective failure recovery mechanism for Web services can be based on the ideas from both database systems and mobile computing. A key step towards such a mechanism is to define what failures are in Web service interaction environment and provide a clear taxonomy for all these failures.

References

1. American National Standards Institute: Study Group on Data Base Management Systems. Interim report, FDT, 7:2, ACM, 1975.
2. Report of the CODASYL Data Base Task Group. ACM, April 1971.
3. M. S. Ackerman. Privacy in E-Commerce: Examining User Scenarios and Privacy Preferences. In *Proceedings of the ACM Conference on Electronic Commerce*, 1999.
4. G. Alonso, F. Casati, H. Kuno, and V. Machiraju. *Web Services: Concepts, Architecture, and Applications*. Springer Verlag, June 2003.
5. M. Astrahan, M. Blasgen, D Chamberlin, K. Eswaran, P. Griffiths J. Gray, F. King III, R. Lorie, P. McJones, J. Mehl, G. Putzolu, I. Traiger, B. Wade, and V. Watson. System R: Relational Approach to Database Management. *ACM Transactions on Database Systems*, 1(2):97–137, 1976.
6. D. Baker, D. Georgakopoulos, H. Schuster, A. R. Cassandra, and A. Cichocki. Providing customized process and situation awareness in the collaboration management infrastructure. In *Proceedings of the Fourth IFCIS International Conference on Cooperative Information Systems, Edinburgh, Scotland, September 2-4, 1999*, pages 79–91. IEEE Computer Society, 1999.
7. F. Barbon, P. Traverso, M. Pistore, and M. Trainotti. Run-time monitoring of instances and classes of web service compositions. In *ICWS '06: Proceedings of the IEEE International Conference on Web Services*, pages 63–71, Washington, DC, USA, 2006. IEEE Computer Society.
8. N. Beckmann, H.-P. Kriegel, R. Schneider, and B. Seeger. The r*-tree: an efficient and robust access method for points and rectangles. In *SIGMOD '90: Proceedings of the 1990 ACM SIGMOD International Conference on Management of Data*, pages 322–331, New York, NY, USA, 1990. ACM.
9. B. Benatallah, F. Casati, D. Grigori, H. R. Motahari Nezhad, and F. Toumani. Developing Adapters for Web Services Integration. In *CAiSE Conference*, pages 415–429, Porto, Portugal, June 2005.
10. B. Benatallah, M. Dumas, M. Sheng, and A. H. H. Ngu. Declarative Composition and Peer-to-Peer Provisioning of Dynamic Web Services. In *ICDE '01: Proceedings of the 17th International Conference on Data Engineering*, pages 297–308, San Jose, California, USA, February 2002.
11. B. Benatallah, Q. Z. Sheng, and M. Dumas. The Self-Serv Environment for Web Services Composition. *IEEE Internet Computing*, 7(1):40–48, 2003.
12. D. Berardi, D. Calvanese, G. De Giacomo, R. Hull, and M. Mecella. Automatic composition of transition-based semantic web services with messaging. In *VLDB '05: Proceedings of the 31st International Conference on Very Large Data Bases*, pages 613–624. VLDB Endowment, 2005.

13. Stefan Berchtold, Daniel A. Keim, and Hans-Peter Kriegel. The x-tree : An index structure for high-dimensional data. In *VLDB'96, Proceedings of 22th International Conference on Very Large Data Bases, September 3-6, 1996, Mumbai (Bombay), India*, pages 28–39. Morgan Kaufmann, 1996.

14. S. Börzsönyi, D. Kossmann, and K. Stocker. The skyline operator. In *ICDE '01: Proceedings of the 17th International Conference on Data Engineering*, pages 421–430, Washington, DC, USA, 2001. IEEE Computer Society.

15. P. Bosc and O. Pivert. SQLf: a relational database language for fuzzy querying. *IEEE Transactions on Fuzzy Systems*, 3(1):1–17, 1995.

16. M. Burstein, C. Bussler, T. Finin, M. Huhns, M. Paolucci, A. Sheth, and S. Williams. A Semantic Web Services Architecture. *IEEE Internet Computing*, 9:52–61, September-October 2005.

17. C. Bussler. B2B Protocal Standards and their Role in Semantic B2B Integration Engines. *IEEE Data Engineering Bulletin*, 24(1), 2001.

18. C. Bussler, D. Fensel, and A. Maedche. A Conceptual Architecture for Semantic Web Enabled Web Services. *SIGMOD Record*, 31(4), December 2002.

19. J. Cardoso. *Quality of service and semantic composition of workflows*. Ph.D Thesis, University of Georgia, Athens, GA, 2002.

20. F. Casati, E. Shan, U. Dayal, and M. Shan. Business-oriented management of web services. *Communications of the ACM*, 46(10):55–60, October 2003.

21. D. Chakerian and D. Logothetti. Cube Slices, Pictorial Triangles, and Probability. *Mathematics Magazine*, 64(4):219–241, 1991.

22. C. Y. Chan, H. V. Jagadish, K. L. Tan, A. K. H. Tung, and Z. Zhang. Finding k-dominant skylines in high dimensional space. In *SIGMOD '06: Proceedings of the 2006 ACM SIGMOD International Conference on Management of Data*, pages 503–514, New York, NY, USA, 2006. ACM.

23. Y.-C. Chang, L. Bergman, V. Castelli, C.-S. Li, M.-L. Lo, and J. R. Smith. The onion technique: indexing for linear optimization queries. *SIGMOD Rec.*, 29(2):391–402, 2000.

24. S. Chaudhuri. An overview of query optimization in relational systems. In *PODS '98: Proceedings of the seventeenth ACM SIGACT-SIGMOD-SIGART Symposium on Principles of Database Systems*, pages 34–43, New York, NY, USA, 1998. ACM.

25. S. Chaudhuri, N. Dalvi, and R. Kaushik. Robust cardinality and cost estimation for skyline operator. In *ICDE '06: Proceedings of the 22nd International Conference on Data Engineering*, page 64, Washington, DC, USA, 2006. IEEE Computer Society.

26. J. Chomicki, P. Godfrey, J.Gryz, and D. Liang. Skyline with presorting. In *ICDE '03: Proceedings of the 19th International Conference on Data Engineering*, pages 717–719, 2003.

27. E. Codd. A relational model for large shared data banks. *Communication of the ACM*, 13(6), 1970.

28. S. Cohen, W. Nutt, and A. Serebrenik. Rewriting aggregate queries using views. In *PODS '99: Proceedings of the eighteenth ACM SIGMOD-SIGACT-SIGART Symposium on Principles of Database Systems*, pages 155–166, New York, NY, USA, 1999. ACM.

29. M. Conti, M. Kumar, S. K. Das, and B. A. Shirazi. Quality of Service Issues in Internet Web Services. *IEEE Transactions on Computers*, 51(6):593 – 594, 2002.

30. Y. Ding, D. Fensel, and and B. Omelayenko M. Klein. The Semantic Web: Yet Another Hip? *Data and Knowledge Engineering*, 41(3):205–227, May 2002.

31. J. Domingue, S. Galizia, and L. Cabral. Choreography in IRS-III - Coping with Heterogeneous Interaction Patterns in Web Services. In *The International Symposium on Wearable Computers*, pages 415–429, Galway, Ireland, November 2005.

32. X. Dong, A. Y. Halevy, J. Madhavan, E. Nemes, and J. Zhang. Similarity search for web services. In *VLDB '04: Proceedings of the Thirtieth International Conference on Very Large Data Bases*, pages 372–383. VLDB Endowment, 2004.

33. D. Fensel and C. Bussler. The Web Service Modeling Framework WSMF. *Electronic Commerce: Research and Applications*, pages 113–137, 2002.
34. H. Garcia-Molina. The TSIMMIS Project: Integration of Heterogeneous Information Sources. *J. Intelligent Information Systems*, 8(2):117–132, May 1997.
35. D. Geer. Taking steps to secure web services. *IEEE Computer*, 36(10):14–16, 2003.
36. D. Georgakopoulos, H. Schuster, A. Chichocki, and D. Baker. Managing process and service fusion in virtual enterprises. *Inf. Syst.*, 24(6):429–456, 1999.
37. P. Godfrey, R. Shipley, and J. Gryz. Maximal vector computation in large data sets. In *VLDB '05: Proceedings of the 31st International Conference on Very Large Data Bases*, pages 229–240. VLDB Endowment, 2005.
38. L. Gravano and Y. Papakonstantinou. Mediating and metasearching on the Internet. *IEEE Data Engineering Bulletin*, 21(2), 1998.
39. Ashish Gupta, Venky Harinarayan, and Dallan Quass. Aggregate-query processing in data warehousing environments. In *VLDB '95: Proceedings of the 21th International Conference on Very Large Data Bases*, pages 358–369, San Francisco, CA, USA, 1995. Morgan Kaufmann Publishers Inc.
40. Alon Y. Halevy, Anand Rajaraman, and Joann J. Ordille. Data integration: the teenage years. In *VLDB '06: Proceedings of the 32nd International Conference on Very Large Data Bases*, pages 9–16. VLDB Endowment, 2006.
41. R. Hamadi and B. Benatallah. A petri net-based model for web service composition. In *Fourteenth Australasian Database Conference on Database Technologies*, pages 191–200, 2003.
42. V. Hristidis, N. Koudas, and Y. Papakonstantinou. Prefer: a system for the efficient execution of multi-parametric ranked queries. *SIGMOD Rec.*, 30(2):259–270, 2001.
43. IBM. *Web Services Conceptual Architecture*. http://www-306.ibm.com/software/solutions /webservices/pdf/WSCA.pdf.
44. IBM. http://www.research.ibm.com/ssme/, 2006.
45. C. Jin, K. Yi, L. Chen, J. X. Yu, and X. Lin. chapter-window top-k queries on uncertain streams. In *VLDB '08: Proceedings of the 33rd International Conference on Very Large Data Bases*. VLDB Endowment, 2008.
46. R. Jurca, B. Faltings, and W. Binder. Reliable qos monitoring based on client feedback. In *WWW '07: Proceedings of the 16th International Conference on World Wide Web*, pages 1003–1012, New York, NY, USA, 2007. ACM.
47. D. Kossmann, F. Ramsak, and S. Rost. Shooting stars in the sky: an online algorithm for skyline queries. In *VLDB '02: Proceedings of the 28th International Conference on Very Large Data Bases*, pages 275–286. VLDB Endowment, 2002.
48. C. S. Langdon. The State of Web Services. *IEEE Computer*, 36(7):93–94, 2003.
49. F. Laymann. Jump Onto The Bus: A Guided Tour To The WS-* Landscape. In *ICSOC '03: Proceedings of the First International Conference on Service-Oriented Computing*. SpringerVerlag, 2003.
50. C. P. Martin and K. Ramamritham. Recovery guarantees in mobile systems. In *Proceedings of the 1st ACM international workshop on Data engineering for wireless and mobile access*, pages 22–28. ACM Press, 1999.
51. E. M. Maximilien and M. P. Singh. A framework and ontology for dynamic web services selection. *IEEE Internet Computing*, 8(5):84–93, 2004.
52. S. A. Mcllraith, T. C. Son, and H. Zeng. Semantic Web services. *IEEE Intelligent Systems*, 16(2):46–53, 2001.
53. B. Medjahed, B. Benatallah, A. Bouguettaya, A. H. H. Ngu, and A. K. Elmagarmid. Business-to-business interactions: issues and enabling technologies. *The VLDB Journal*, 12(1):59–85, 2003.
54. B. Medjahed and A. Bouguettaya. A Multilevel Composability Model for Semantic Web Services. *IEEE Transaction on Knowledge and Data Engineering (TKDE)*, 17(7):954–968, July 2005.
55. B. Medjahed, A. Bouguettaya, and A. K. Elmagarmid. Composing Web Services on the Semantic Web. *VLDB Journal*, 12(4), November 2003.

56. B. Medjahed, A. Rezgui, A. Bouguettaya, and M. Ouzzani. Infrastructure for E-Government Web Services. *IEEE Internet Computing*, 7(1):58–65, 2003.

57. Nuno Neves and W. Kent Fuchs. Adaptive recovery for mobile environments. *Commun. ACM*, 40(1):68–74, 1997.

58. OASIS. *Universal Description, Discovery, and Integration (UDDI)*. http://www.uddi.org.

59. M. Ouzzani and B. Bouguettaya. Efficient Access to Web Services. *IEEE Internet Computing*, 37(3), March 2004.

60. D. Papadias, Y. Tao, G. Fu, and B. Seeger. An optimal and progressive algorithm for skyline queries. In *SIGMOD '03: Proceedings of the 2003 ACM SIGMOD International Conference on Management of Data*, pages 467–478, New York, NY, USA, 2003. ACM.

61. M. P. Papazoglou and J. Dubray. A Survey of Web service technologies. Technical Report DIT-04-058, University of Trento, 2004.

62. M.P. Papazoglou and W.-J. van den Heuvel. Web Services Management: A Survey. *IEEE Internet Computing*, pages 58–64, 2005.

63. J. Pei, B. Jiang, X. Lin, and Y. Yuan. Probabilistic skylines on uncertain data. In *VLDB '07: Proceedings of the 33rd International Conference on Very Large Data Bases*, pages 15–26. VLDB Endowment, 2007.

64. J. Pei, W. Jin, M. Ester, and Y. Tao. Catching the best views of skyline: a semantic approach based on decisive subspaces. In *VLDB '05: Proceedings of the 31st International Conference on Very Large Data Bases*, pages 253–264. VLDB Endowment, 2005.

65. C. Petrie and C. Bussler. Service Agents and Virtual Enterprises: A Survey. *IEEE Internet Computing*, 7(4):68–78, 2003.

66. R. Prakash and M. Singhal. Low-cost checkpointing and failure recovery in mobile computing systems. *IEEE Trans. Parallel Distrib. Syst.*, 7(10):1035–1048, 1996.

67. K. Pu, V. Hristidis, and N. Koudas. In *ICDE '06: Proceedings of the 22nd International Conference on Data Engineering*, page 31, Washington, DC, USA, 2006. IEEE Computer Society.

68. A. Rezgui, A. Bouguettaya, and M. Y. Eltoweissy. Privacy on the Web: Facts, Challenges, and Solutions. *IEEE Security&Privacy*, 1(6):40–49, 2003.

69. J. Riordan. *An Introduction to Combinatorial Analysis*. John Wiley and Sons, Inc, New York, 1958.

70. Nick Roussopoulos, Stephen Kelley, and Frédéric Vincent. Nearest neighbor queries. In *SIGMOD '95: Proceedings of the 1995 ACM SIGMOD International Conference on Management of Data*, pages 71–79, New York, NY, USA, 1995. ACM.

71. P. Selinger, M.M. Astrahanand, D.D. Chamberlin, R.A. Lorie, and T.G. Price. Access path selection in a relational database management system. In *SIGMOD '79: Proceedings of the 1979 ACM SIGMOD International Conference on Management of Data*, pages 23–34, New York, NY, USA, 1979. ACM.

72. M. P. Singh and M. N. Huhns. *Service-Oriented Computing Semantics, Processes, Agents*. John Wiley & Sons, Ltd., 2005.

73. E. Sirin, J. Hendler, and B. Parsia. Semi-automatic composition of web services using semantic descriptions. In *Web Services: Modeling, Architecture and Infrastructure workshop in conjunction with ICEIS2003*, 2003.

74. J. Spohrer and D. Riecken editors. Special issue on services science. *Commun. ACM*, 49(7), July 2006.

75. Divesh Srivastava, Shaul Dar, H. V. Jagadish, and Alon Y. Levy. Answering queries with aggregation using views. In *VLDB '96: Proceedings of the 22th International Conference on Very Large Data Bases*, pages 318–329, San Francisco, CA, USA, 1996. Morgan Kaufmann Publishers Inc.

76. U. Srivastava, J. Widom, K. Munagala, and R. Motwani. Query optimization over web services. In *VLDB '06: Proceedings of the 32nd International Conference on Very Large Data Bases*, pages 355–366. VLDB Endowment, 2006.

77. M. Stonebraker, E. Wong, P. Kreps, and G. Held. The design and implementation of ingres. *ACM Transactions on Database Systems*, 1(3), 1976.

78. Dave D. Straube and M. Tamer Özsu. Query optimization and execution plan generation in object-oriented data management systems. *IEEE Trans. Knowl. Data Eng.*, 7(2):210–227, 1995.

79. Systinet. *Systinet Server for Java*. http://www.systinet.com/products/ssj/overview, 2004.

80. K.-L. Tan, P.-K. Eng, and B. C. Ooi. Efficient progressive skyline computation. In *VLDB '01: Proceedings of the 27th International Conference on Very Large Data Bases*, pages 301–310, San Francisco, CA, USA, 2001. Morgan Kaufmann Publishers Inc.

81. Y. Tao, X. Xiao, and J. Pei. Subsky: Efficient computation of skylines in subspaces. In *ICDE '06: Proceedings of the 22nd International Conference on Data Engineering*, page 65, Washington, DC, USA, 2006. IEEE Computer Society.

82. A. Tsalgatidou and T. Pilioura. An Overview of Standards and Related Technology in Web Services. *Distributed and Parallel Databases*, 12(2):135–162, 2002.

83. S. J. Vaughan-Nichols. Web services: Beyond the hype. *IEEE Computer*, 35(2):18–21, 2002.

84. S. Vinoski. Web services interaction models, part 1: Current Practice. *IEEE Internet Computing*, 6(3):89–91, 2002.

85. W3C. *Simple Object Access Protocol (SOAP)*. http://www.w3.org/TR/soap.

86. W3C. *Web Service Execution Environment (WSMX)*. http://www.w3.org/Submission/WSMX/.

87. W3C. *Web Services Description Language (WSDL)*. http://www.w3.org/TR/wsdl.

88. W3C. Web Services Architecture. *http://www.w3.org/TR/ws-arch/*, 2003.

89. Workflow Management Coalition. Workflow Management Application Programming Interface (Interface 2&3) Specification. Document Number WFMC-TC-1009, July 1998. Version 2.0.

90. WS-I. *Web Services Interoperability Organization.* http://www.ws-i.org/.

91. J. Yang. Web Service Componentization. *Communications of the ACM*, 46(10):35–40, 2003.

92. T. Yu, Y. Zhang, and K. J. Lin. Efficient algorithms for web services selection with end-to-end qos constraints. *ACM Trans. Web*, 1(1), 2007.

93. Y. Yuan, X. Lin, Q. Liu, W. Wang, J. Xu Yu, and Q. Zhang. Efficient computation of the skyline cube. In *VLDB '05: Proceedings of the 31st International Conference on Very Large Data Bases*, pages 241–252. VLDB Endowment, 2005.

94. L. Zeng, B. Benatallah, M. Dumas, J. Kalagnanam, and Q. Sheng. Quality driven web services composition. In *WWW '03: Proceedings of the 12th international conference on World Wide Web*, pages 411–421, New York, NY, USA, 2003. ACM.

95. L. Zeng, B. Benatallah, A.H.H. Ngu, M. Dumas, J. Kalagnanam, and H. Chang. Qos-aware middleware for web services composition. *IEEE Trans. Softw. Eng.*, 30(5):311–327, 2004.

Index

Breinigsville, PA USA
25 June 2010
240424BV00006B/73/P